Church Growth Under Fire

Church Growth Under Fire

C. WAYNE ZUNKEL

HERALD PRESS
Scottdale, Pennsylvania
Kitchener, Ontario
1987

Library of Congress Cataloging-in-Publication Data

Zunkel, C. Wayne, 1931-
   Church growth under fire.

   Bibliography: p.
   Includes indexes.
   1. Church growth.   2. Church growth—Controversial
literature.   I. Title.
BV652.25.Z858   1987   254'.5   86-31814
ISBN 0-8361-3428-1 (pbk.)

Scripture references designated RSV are from the Revised
Standard Version of the Bible, copyrighted 1946, 1952, © 1971,
1973.

Scripture references designated TEV are from the *Good News
Bible.* Old Testament, copyright © American Bible Society 1976;
New Testament copyright © American Bible Society 1966, 1971,
1976.

Scripture references designated LB or "The Living Bible" are
from *The Living Bible, Paraphrased* (Wheaton: Tyndale House
Publishers, 1971) and are used by permission.

CHURCH GROWTH UNDER FIRE
Copyright © 1987 by C. Wayne Zunkel
Published by Herald Press, Scottdale, Pa. 15683
    Released simultaneously in Canada by Herald Press,
    Kitchener, Ont. N2G 4M5. All rights reserved.
Library of Congress Catalog Card Number: 86-31814
International Standard Book Number: 0-8361-3428-1
Printed in the United States of America
Cover illustration by Joel Kauffmann
Cartoon art and illustrations by Cathy Earhart
Design by Gwen M. Stamm

87 88 89 90 91 92 9 8 7 6 5 4 3 2 1

· · · · · · · · · ·

Dedicated to Christian heroes in every age
　　whose lives disturbed and challenged and healed us,
　　who refused to settle for half a Christ:
　　people like . . .
　　Jesus' mother, *Mary*, who in her song of praise to
　　　　God her Savior,
　　　　acknowledged his mercy toward the lowly,
　　　　his justice for the poor and oppressed;
　　Francis of Assisi, whose conversion came as he dis-
　　　　mounted his horse to embrace a poor leper,
　　　　and who devoted his life to Jesus and to Lady
　　　　Poverty;
　　Menno Simons, whose understanding of the church
　　　　made him a hunted man;
　　John Wesley, evangelist of fire,
　　　　who gave a clear proclamation of personal salva-
　　　　tion, but who did not hesitate to deal with such
　　　　topics as wealth, war, education, medical ethics,
　　　　prison reform;
　　Christopher Sauer, a printer in Colonial days, above
　　　　whose shop was the sign "For the Glory of God
　　　　and My Neighbor's Good";
　　John Greenleaf Whittier, author of "Dear Lord and
　　　　Father of Mankind" and opponent of slavery
　　　　who was pelted with eggs for his strong ser-
　　　　mons;
　　Mother Teresa, working among the poorest of the
　　　　poor in Calcutta;
　　Corrie ten Boom, Albert Schweitzer, Pope John XXIII,
　　　　and a host of *black* and *third world pastors
　　　　and leaders.*
　　And the list goes on . . .

Contents

Preface

At my denomination's annual conference in 1986, the delegates were discussing the church's response to the tragic events in South Africa between whites and blacks. One delegate rose to say, "I am not concerned about all of that. All that matters to me is the great commission." As she talked, I thought, "Where has she been? The great commission talks of 'making disciples of all peoples.' It talks of 'teaching them to observe *all* that I have commanded you' " (Matthew 28:19-20).

How on God's good earth could anyone claim to care about the great commission and not care about God's hurting people?

I think of other church members I know.

The Reverend Shin Keun Kim at age 73 heads a 6000-student elementary, junior high, and senior high school in Kwang-Ju, Korea. He is a magnificent man with a ready smile and boundless energy. During his lifetime he established some 18 congregations. On a trip to Israel in 1960, he was impressed by the kibutzim. Returning to Korea, Rev. Kim (as the Koreans call him) tried to interest officials in his country in the concept, but without success. So he went out and did it himself. He bought some reclaimed land—land formerly under water—six kilometers by two kilometers. He built a village of 22 duplex cinder block homes with a church at the center.

Poor farmers from the area were invited to be a part of the experiment. In time they would own their homes and the land. He bought 900 cattle from the United States, kept 160 for his village, and gave the rest to poor villages nearby. He calls the farm and the school *Soong Eu*, which means "righteousness" or "justice."

While visiting his "farm," Rev. Kim told me that as a young man he had been a student in Japan. Late one night he saw a group of Japanese young men beating up a Korean student. He took off his shoes and began hitting the Japanese with the heels of his shoes to drive them off. He confided to me that from that day on he vowed he would never speak the Japanese language again.

He became a part of the independence movement against the Japanese occupation of his country and was imprisoned. Once he got in a scuffle with a Japanese guard in the prison. But he kept his vow never to speak Japanese.

But on his 1960 trip to Israel he saw a group of Orientals ahead. Thinking they were Koreans, he went running to them. When he discovered they were Japanese, suddenly he realized the foolishness of the hatred he had been carrying all those years. He discarded his hatred and learned to love his enemies.

After visiting Rev. Kim in Kwang-Ju, I went to Kobe, Japan. I spent a week with Japanese pastors in a workshop sponsored by the Japan Church Growth Institute. The last night there, the phone in my room rang. I had gone to bed and was asleep. It was Ishikawa, one of the Japanese pastors, wanting to talk with me. He told me he had served in World War II against America and hated Americans at that time. He also hated the Christian religion. Along the way his life was turned around. He accepted Christ and his life was changed.

Now he was seeking to cross other barriers of hatred. He had traveled up and down Japan to recruit 300 Japanese pastors to visit Korea. Many Japanese look upon Koreans with contempt. Yet the Korean church is flourishing while the size of the average Japanese congregation is 29. Pastor Ishikawa wanted to take a delegation of Japanese pastors to Korea to live for three months, to sleep in dormitories, to live on rice and soup, to study and pray, and to learn from the Koreans about building Christ's church.

Knowing Christ had freed Japanese and Korean Christians to reach across painful barriers that had existed for a thousand years.

We often divide "saving souls" and "caring for human needs." We divide preaching Christ and following Christ. But many in our world know that to preach Christ is not only to proclaim a name but to uphold a Person and all that that Person asked of us.

I think of my own father. From day one he presented the gospel as both social and personal.

My pastor father was always evangelistic, winning and incorporating new people into the body of Christ. He spent long hours with people who were struggling and lost. While on the staff at our national headquarters, he was instrumental in the launching of 77 new congregations, many of them today, thirty years later, among the largest and strongest in our denomination. The congregations he served grew. Lives were changed.

Yet he never hesitated to speak and act on the wider imperatives of the gospel. He believed God loves individuals. He also took seriously John 3:16: "God so loved the *world. . . .*" Not just the church. Not just the "saved." The world.

In Wenatchee, Washington, during World War II a Japanese-American family was forcibly removed from their home to be taken to a "relocation" camp. The church my father pastored moved in to assure that their home and furnishings would be there when they returned.

In that amazing church was a businessman, Ross Heminger, who built the young couples' class. After a tiring day he would come home exhausted. He said nothing refreshed him after his evening meal so much as to get into his car and visit couples he was incorporating into the life of that church.

During the Depression, other packinghouse owners had announced to the growers and workers, "30 cents on the dollar, take it or leave it." This businessman and his family moved to turn their packing shed over to the growers as a cooperative where all shared in the profits and the losses.

During World War II in Lima, Ohio, an industrial town called "Little Chicago," my father preached his conviction that "all war is sin." My music teacher was the paid choir director at church. I remember going for a lesson and standing a few steps back while my respected music teacher, livid with rage, called my father names I had never heard before because my dad loved Germans and Japanese, even in the midst of war.

But long before even that, I am grateful for a Christ who felt equally at home in challenging corrupt political machines as he walked into the temple to overturn the tables of moneychangers in a system which required the very poor to give to ruling officials what the poor did not have (Matthew 21:12-13). And with the same passion I see my Lord stopping to touch the eyes of a man born blind (Mark 8:23) or to release from sin a woman married five times and living now with a sixth man who was not her husband (John 4:18).

It is against this backdrop and with these convictions that I write. *We must again restore the unity of the gospel.* The Christian faith cares about individuals and their sin *and* about the gross sin and brokenness which individuals visit upon each other. Christ would free us from both.

I write, grateful to a whole host of Christians from the time of Jesus of Nazareth to our own who have embodied a truly full gospel.

I write with special debt to Christians I have known

who have refused to let the gospel be divided. I write with a debt of thanks to people in the Church Growth Movement and at Fuller Theological Seminary, and especially to Peter Wagner, a major professor at Fuller for me, who encouraged and supported me as I tried to relate my own understandings of faith to the marvelous insights of Donald McGavran and those of the modern Church Growth Movement.

It is with these biases and with this debt of thanks that I write.

C. Wayne Zunkel

Chapter 1 ·

Cheap Grace and Church Growth

The apostle Paul put it in stirring terms: "You know," he wrote in 1 Thessalonians 2:11-12, "like a father talking to his own boy, we counseled with each one of you, sharing our insight and showing you how to walk becomingly of the God who called us *into his movement and magnificence.*"[1]

The vision is too grand, the call is too sweeping, the charge too important to be cheapened by gimmicks or shallow sales schemes.

On our hearts has been placed a mandate which involves all of God's creation. And God himself calls us to the task.

He wants his children to know that it is indeed his world. He wants them to live knowing each other and knowing him. Jesus Christ is the window ... to others and to God. He is humanity's idea of God. He is God's idea of humanity. And we are the ambassadors. The vehicle for sharing this passion of the heart of the Father is the church. It is to be the new community set in the midst of the old.

Jesus has given us license to play heaven on this dirty earth. We are called to be a living example of his life in the midst of death and decay. Tomorrow now. Realized eschatology.[2]

But little people grasp only part of the dream. In their

15

eagerness to share it, they leave much out. They use cheap methods for a priceless message.

Late one April evening in 1985, for several hours I walked the city streets of Seoul, Korea, with Sang Bong Kim, a frail and sensitive professor of religion at a university there. We walked past a huge church, still under construction. My young friend paused by the enormous building and said, "That represents some of the best in rapid church growth so evident in Korea." He paused and then added, "It also represents the shallowness of far too much of the Christian church here." As he talked, he indicated that at times he felt Christians had traded depth for rapid growth.

Or, as they say in business economics, when the price goes down, the number sold tends to go up.[3]

Karl Barth, discussing church growth, would have us ask, "Is it merely a question, as in other human societies, of . . . drawing large crowds and thus enjoying success?" The growth God seeks "is the growth in virtue of a power absolutely distinctive to the community of saints." Barth warns: "It can never be healthy if the Church seeks to grow only or predominantly in [a] horizontal sense, with a view to the greatest possible number of adherents; if its mission to the world becomes propaganda on behalf of its own spatial expansion."

At all points our task is to "attest the Gospel . . . to seek a hearing and understanding for the Gospel's voice." Always "it will have to resist the temptation to win them by *diluting the wine with a little water.*"[4]

After nearly 40 years of research and study of church growth worldwide, a group of U.S. pastors asked if these worldwide principles did not also apply in the States. A course team-taught by Donald McGavran and Peter Wagner at Lake Avenue Congregational Church in Pasadena was the first introduction to the American church setting in 1972.

Greeting the first wave of interest was a book by

Richard Hudnut bluntly entitled *Church Growth Is Not the Point.* His concern was a renewed and faithful remnant. "There are men and women serving pulpits all over America who refuse to huckster Christ," he wrote, "who are dead serious about the claims the Suffering Servant makes upon them...."

Having just come through the 60s (which was really about 1964 to 1974) and their dramatic loss of church membership, Hudnut wrote, "Loss of growth in statistics has often meant increase in growth in the Gospel." For him it meant that "the 'dead wood' is gone. The 'faithful remnant' remains. The church is lean and stripped for action."[5]

In my own experience I learned to talk with pride about how we had fewer members and fewer in attendance, but far greater dedication as the budget at the church I served went in three brief years from $17,000 a year to nearly $70,000.

Elton Trueblood, writing about *The Incendiary Fellowship,* spoke a truth substantiated by many strands in the Scriptures: "We are far more effective if we know that the Gospel will never be entirely acceptable, and that the Christian Movement will continue to be a minority movement." Unfortunately, when I first read that book in the 1960s, I failed to notice the next sentence of that paragraph: "The Gospel must seek to penetrate the world and all its parts, but it cannot do so unless there is a sense in which it is in contrast to the world. Herein lies the central paradox."[6]

The former pastor of Glendale, California's largest church, the "Methodist Cathedral of the West," once told me, "I, too, could grow a church if I saw a vision of a 900-foot-tall Christ, or was willing to resort to cheap promotion, or would run our congregation like a tight-fisted dictator."

A former pastor of one of the small churches I serve said to me as we sat at lunch one day, "You and I both know how we could fill that church. Preach a popular gospel. Preach shallow nationalism with a vocabulary of well-worn religious words. Water it down and people will come pouring in."

Dietrich Bonhoeffer, a German Christian who at age 39, just four weeks before the conclusion of World War II, was

HURRY OR YOU'LL NEVER MAKE IT!

hanged for his unrelenting opposition to the Nazis, smuggled his ideas out of prison on scraps of paper. He used the phrase "cheap grace."[7] A Lutheran, he was saddened and angered by the willingness of so many Christians in Germany to fall into obedient step behind Adolf Hitler.

Bonhoeffer, in the middle phase of his life (each was distinct and different in emphasis),[8] talked of discipleship—of the willingness to follow Jesus just as Simon Peter in the first century heard Christ call, left his nets, "burned his boats" (to use Bonhoeffer's phrase), and followed him. We are to go, *not knowing* where he will take us or what it will mean. We give over absolute allegiance to this Person. And it is a costly road.

It is not a call to a creed nor to a set of ethics first of all, but a call to "come follow," without knowing the outcome.

Perhaps nowhere is it more beautifully expressed than in those familiar words of Albert Schweitzer:

> He comes to us as one unknown, without a name, as of old by the lakeside he came to those men who knew him not. He speaks to us the same word, "Follow thou me," and sets us to the tasks which he has to fulfill for our time. He commands. And to those who obey, whether they be wise or simple, he will reveal himself in the toils, the conflicts, the suffering which they shall pass through in his fellowship, and as an ineffable mystery, they shall learn in their own experience who he is.[9]

So easily we slip over into an attempt to build our empires. Bonhoeffer warns, "The Church has neither the wish nor the obligation to extend her space to cover the space of the world. She asks for no more space than she needs for the purpose of serving the world by bearing witness to Jesus Christ and to the reconciliation of the world with God through Him." And always "one must bear in mind that the confines of this space are at every moment being overrun and broken down by the testimony of the church to Jesus Christ."[10]

Bonhoeffer's renewed call to costly, responsible discipleship cannot be ignored.

Taking our cue from Bonhoeffer's phrase, I would have you explore with me a modern rediscovery of some very old truths. To some, the growing interest in church growth is a violation of the best of our faith. To others it is a *rediscovery* of exciting aspects of our faith seen first in the New Testament. But our look together in this volume will be at *cheap grace and church growth.* To state it as a question: Can the insights of the modern Church Growth movement be reconciled with the *costly* grace seen in the New Testament? Do Church Growth principles measure up to the high quality of the "movement and magnificence" into which we are called?

And finally, we want to ask, How does it all apply to you and me and to the congregations in which our own Christian life is rooted? Our interest is not simply in abstract arguments but in life and death questions which must come down finally to real flesh-and-blood situations.

We will try to let it find direct application to where we worship, where we work, where we live.

Chapter 2 ·

With a Bad Name

The Church Growth movement is hot. An ever increasing number of Christians—lay and clergy—are becoming fascinated with it. Many pastors find in it insight which bring together some of their personal findings from many fields. They find here a solid basis for knowing which hunches to pursue and which guesses are dead-end streets. Here there is some intelligent basis for knowing what strategies to discard and what to retain. In my own ministry, I have found the movement "naming" discoveries onto which I myself had stumbled, giving them direction and focus.

Many lay people—liberal and conservative—are intrigued by it. Conservatives—because the hope that the church will concern itself more directly with evangelism has long been in their hearts and on their lips. Liberals—because the approach to Church Growth strikes a responsive chord and matches efforts in other secular fields. It brings thoughtful procedures to an area of faith which they naggingly suspect they have been neglecting.

But many church leaders are uneasy. For some, Church Growth as a movement and church growth as a goal have been dismissed out of hand. It is important that we examine the *criticisms* and the *movement* and see what each has to say to the other.

Some of the criticism comes from friendly, informed adversaries. Some who have read the material have entered into serious dialogue with Church Growth proponents. Mennonite scholar John Howard Yoder says frankly that for him *"criticism does not mean rejection"* (the italics are his). But he finds areas where his own understanding of the gospel raises serious questions about some of the implications of the principles which "the movement" has spelled out.[1] Such concerns merit careful consideration.

Other criticisms come from equally sincere persons who care deeply about what they perceive to be a threat to something precious, but whose knowledge of Church Growth is from critics of the movement, not from the Church Growth literature itself.

With great eagerness I began to read an article on the "Dangers of the Church Growth Movement" in *The Christian Century.*[2] The author said, "I bought every book and I read every manual on the subject. Now I am more concerned than ever because I believe this movement to be one of the worst distortions of the church that American ingenuity born of an outworn capitalist mentality ... could possibly devise."

As I read, I felt in harmony with the writer's basic concerns. But his understanding of Church Growth seemed like what happens when I get carbon paper in with the wrong side up: correct in every detail, but backwards.

I myself had come to Church Growth as a skeptic, as indeed have many others. Peter Wagner, perhaps the leading exponent, confesses that after first reading some of Donald McGavran's works on the mission field, he put them on the area of his mission station home relegated to "termite food."

I could understand the skepticism. I had trouble when I saw basic misunderstandings or misstatements of what people like Wagner and McGavran were saying.[3]

But even these criticisms need to be faced honestly and openly, one by one.

One of the things that has attracted me, I must confess, has been the "openness" of Peter Wagner and other faculty at Fuller Theological Seminary, which is the center of much of the ferment.

When a critic like John Howard Yoder questioned their assumptions, they invited him to campus for several days to enter into dialogue.

The leading critics of the homogeneous principle also were invited and spent several days sharing their views— not to be convinced, but to help the "movement" become more true to the gospel it seeks to share.

It is a sheer delight to see the response of Peter Wagner to correction or criticism. Someone will challenge an assumption in a thoughtful way and he will respond with his wonderful laughter and say with obvious pleasure, "Isn't that just great!" He rejoices at valid correction of his views the way I rejoice when I have scored a point in an argument.

To see the theoreticians in the flesh helps too. Knowing something of how faith is lived out by them helps to alter many preconceptions.

When the *Century* article charged Peter Wagner by name with believing that "segregation is the desired end," I knew better, for I knew Wagner.

I personally knew of his involvement in a campaign in his hometown of Pasadena in support of candidates *for* busing to achieve integration in the public schools.

I knew that his own conservative Lake Avenue Congregational Church had 20 black families in membership, 10 Hispanic families, and 10 Asian families. In addition, they had begun a church for Chinese-speaking people and a Filipino church. At "racist" Fuller Seminary, I sat in classes which were as racially and culturally mixed as any experience in my life. Its School of World Mission had students from 50 different nations. There were 100 blacks (more than any other seminary in the country), 80 Hispanics, and 40 Asians.

When Tom Nees reviewed in *Sojourners* Wagner's book, *Our Kind of People*, he titled his review "Evangelism Without the Gospel."[4] I protested to Peter Wagner that it was unfair. His response was to smile and welcome the review, saying, "We need all the criticism and help we can get."

All of this is to admit something of my own pilgrimage and bias. It is also to issue the plea that we evaluate Church Growth as we should evaluate every area—on the basis of what it is rather than on what it isn't.

Part of the pain for me personally is that some of those who are most critical are people I admire very much. Friends personally, and friends from their writings, we have still come to very different conclusions.

Not All Growth Is Good

A favorite professor of my college days put some of the criticism directly. A challenging, concerned, lifelong careful student of religion, Tim (T. Wayne) Rieman wrote bluntly that growth may or may not be good. "*Cancer* is growth—wild, unchecked, out of harmony with the whole being." And, he insists, "Church growth can be cancerous—out of harmony with the Head, Jesus the Christ." How? "When churches stoop to gimmicks, contests, prizes, parachute jumps onto the parking lot, free Burger Chefs for all, competitive busing, stealing members, and a host of other practices like this ... then the church has become a circus."[5]

Tim goes on.

"Not all growth is good. Many have gone the glamour route, turned to show biz, the Hollywood approach; things are suave, smooth, well-oiled, professional."

All fluff and no substance, some would say. "Anything to help churches grow and to get oceans of money."

The real questions, says my professor friend and former teacher, are, "What does Jesus require of us?" and, "How can we convert the church?" The church, he argues, "is *the greatest mission field* in the world: ... unredeemed, unrepentant, unconverted, worldly, smug, classist, untithing, committed to violence, and fundamentally unconcerned about Jesus' favorite people—the poor!" Harsh words.

My dear teacher and friend goes further. "*Should* the church grow?" His response is *"No.* I don't want *this* church to grow! I want it to be redeemed, to be reborn, renewed."

And yet, for all his critical words, Professor Rieman talks of insights found in Ephesians which express the belief "that Jesus and his church will unite all, that the church will heal all divisions, bridge the ideological gaps between the nations ... heal a broken world." Rieman writes, "It seems to me, finally, that what is needed above all else, is to restore the Ephesian hope. Namely, that the church is God's means of doing what needs to be done in the world."

So my critic friend, like so many critic friends, came full circle. Expressing bitter disappointment yet holding onto a New Testament hope, even in spite of what seems to him overwhelming evidence to smother that hope.

Can we, like a farmer driving a team of galloping workhorses, hold fast to both the *good of the criticism* and the *good of what is criticized?* Can we argue for a church that is faithful, insightful, courageous, and dedicated? Can we at the same time argue for a church that reaches out with intelligent passion, informed enthusiasm, to share the riches entrusted to it? Must it be one or the other? Or, in fact, *must* it be *both?* Could it be that Christ has called us both to *be* disciples in the deepest, truest sense, and at the same time to *make* disciples with an unrelenting passion? And might it be that one without the other gets us skewered off into one direction or another which eventually takes us far from the central goal to which we are called? Like an uneven load of wet clothes in a washer that shakes the whole machine and brings it to a complete stop?

Criticisms initially focus in two areas. One has to do with *church*—its value, its importance, its right to any claim upon our allegiance. And the second area of criticism initially has to do with *growth*—whether or not that is a worthy goal.

"Church" Under Fire

It is not strange that the church has its critics.

Strong voices within the church have been its critics.

J. H. Oldham, in a remark to Paul Tillich, states the paradox of faith and frustration. "You know, Tillich," he reports himself as saying, "Christianity has no meaning for me whatsoever apart from the Church. But I sometimes feel as though the church as it actually exists is the source of all my doubts and difficulties."[6]

Karl Barth paints with a poetic, prophetic brush as he describes the church. He puts it in terms of challenge. "*Jesus Christ* first calls certain men out of the common mass and constitutes and maintains them as the community of His witnesses in common adherence to Him." Or again, "*He* is the secret, the basis, the Creator and Lord of the existence of His people. . . . It lives only as He, the Living One, has controlled and still controls it."[7]

Barth goes on to say, "*The community is not Jesus Christ.* . . . It does not 'possess' Him. It cannot create or control Him. It can only receive Him and then be obedient to Him." We are a community of sinful people among others—"saints who are holy only in the fact that He is, and has revealed and disclosed himself" to us and we have "been recognized and confess Him as such."[8]

The community is not Jesus Christ. "*But He*—and in reality only He, but He in supreme reality—*is the community.* He does not live because and as it lives. But it lives, and may and can live, only because and as He lives."

The communion of saints is in danger, says Barth. "It was always in danger. As long as time endures, it will al-

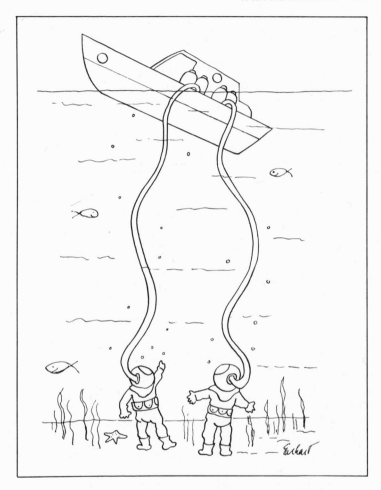

ways be in danger. For it is a human society among men."
He calls it "a provisional representation of the new humanity."

Some in our day question the church and the faith it
represents with a passion. Sheila Thompson dedicated to
the Freedom from Religion Foundation, Inc., talks of how
she was led from religion to unreligion.

"I was brought up as a Missouri Synod Lutheran," she says. "When I was quite young, I had a child out of wedlock. In my anguish, I wrote to an evangelist for help.

"I hoped for a sensitive and personal reply. Instead, I got a pamphlet that, in effect, said: 'You are lucky you were not born 300 years ago. At that time you would have been burned at the stake.'

"That got me to thinking, and I began to read some free-thinking magazines. Eventually, I guess, I got the message."9

Some share the views of screen actor William Hurt, a former theological student for three years, who puts it bluntly. "Christianity is screwed up," he says. "Our representative religion in Western culture is physics."10 "Religion does not represent humanity anymore."11

But for many it is not an angry thing at all. The *mood* contributes. We have come through a period when all institutions have come under fire: Congress, the Supreme Court, the presidency, educational institutions, even the home and marriage.

Why belong to a church? "What difference does a church 'letter'—a piece of paper—make?" many argue. We could ask the same thing when we buy a car or a home, or cash a check, or go to the theater or ball game, or end a week's work. Pieces of paper play a very important role in our lives in virtually every area. In an elusive world, where life keeps moving on, words, symbols, statements of faith or reality, pieces of paper which attest to conditions at a given time and place—all of these are tremendously important. They are markers, street signs, focal points, from which to proceed. Else nothing is nailed down and there never is any meaningful moving on. Without cash in hand after work is completed, the contract between worker and employer is incomplete. Little things—*like paper* money—mean a lot.

Reality forever needs definition. Jacob one night, sleeping in a rocky field while fleeing from his brother Esau, was ministered to by angels of God. He arose to turn one of the stones in that forsaken field upright and proclaim that spot *Beth-el*—the house of God. And "none other than ... the gate of heaven" (Genesis 28:17, RSV). He needed a visible reminder of an invisible and eternal God, an earthly symbol of an eternal reality.

Invading neighbors once broke into the tabernacle to see the Hebrew God. They were stunned to discover that the holy of holies was empty. Nothing was there. It was empty.[12]

But the Hebrews were convinced that their unseen God needed definition, walls—some earthly, human reminder that in the midst of our dirty earth there is a gracious, holy Creator and Redeemer at work.

Our own lives need definition. Or they will spill all over the place.

The truth is we *need* institutions. Without them we don't go far. We could as easily say, "I believe in *baseball* but I oppose institutional baseball. I don't believe in teams or managers or playing fields or stadiums or leagues or rules. Who needs all that? I can play baseball as well on my own."

Or, "I love *learning*. But I don't believe in institutional learning." Of course, there are a few self-taught persons in many fields. If you look you can find them.

But why spend the tens of thousands for a higher education learning experience when you can as well pick up a bibliography (the product of an institution) and go to a public library (itself an institution) and check out the books (produced by a publishing institution) at no cost and educate yourself?

Or, "I love *music*. But I don't want any part of institutional music. Orchestras. Bands. Formal teachers. Music publishing houses. I'll just do it on my own." (What? Create your own instrument? Devise your own scale? Use only your own songs?)

Dogs have few institutions. They have no way of passing on from one generation to the next abstract ideas or detailed facts and discoveries. They may band together for food or defense but little happens beyond that.

Elton Trueblood, calling the church "the company of the committed," wrote that people are "often brave and good alone, but they are never really effective unless they share in some kind of group reality. Voices crying in the wilderness are not permanently recorded."[13]

Institutions are our vehicle for coming together as humans to achieve a purpose. And the church, the synagogue, the *ecclesia*, the "called out," the "gathered" is the institution for achieving God's will in his world.

There is an old story about an aging pastor in a small New England town. Some of the men on the street decided to have fun with the old fellow. One of them asked, "Tell us, preacher, must I belong to the church if I am to go to heaven?"

The old man said in reply, "First let me ask you a question, friend. Could you in one of those boats go from here to England by yourself?"

The fellow thought and said, "I don't know, could I? You tell *me*."

"Yes, I think you could," said the old parson. "If your supplies of water and food held out. If you did not get sick. If you avoided the storms and high waves. If you stayed off the travel lanes. Barring anything unforeseen. But wouldn't it be easier and surer to do it with others together in a larger vessel?"

Our little Jonathan came along almost nine years after our youngest child. We were impressed again at how small babies are. The other children enjoyed him as much as we. Our 17-year-old, David, was amazed: "We have to do everything for him. He can't do anything for himself. Why, he would die if it were not for us."

We need each other is the message of the New Testament. To be saved individually and never folded into the fellowship of the church is like placing a newborn infant in a warm blanket out on the street to raise itself. The chances of survival are as great. But Christ did not call us to new life, plant his impossible dreams in our hearts, and then abandon us like orphans. We have a family to love us, feed us, nourish us, help us first with baby steps and then, with growing confidence, to "grow up in every way into him who is the head" (Ephesians 4:15, RSV).

But this family of ours is so imperfect. They may have been called together by God himself, but there certainly are a lot of clods in the family. Churches may be called to be "colonies of heaven" but they seem to have *amnesia*. Michael Griffiths in his stirring little book, *God's Forgetful Pilgrims: Recalling the Church to Its Reason for Being*, notes the Bible may talk about "the bride of Christ," "but the church today seems like *a ragged Cinderella*, hideous among the ashes."[14]

I was fascinated with events in Spain in the early days of their attempt at democracy. King Juan Carlos struggled to maintain his country's fragile constitutional government. While the masses of church people applauded the courageous king's efforts to successfully turn back an attempt at military takeover on February 23 in 1981, behind the scenes more powerful churchmen, dedicated to the Spain of old, had a part in wanting to destroy the infant attempts at freedom.

The scene could be repeated around the world. Christians at all levels of church life are totally dedicated to righteousness, simple justice. Often in the same land, other church people are just as strong in their unrelenting support of the forces of injustice and oppression.

It happened in Hitler's Germany. Masses of Christians supported Hitler. Clusters of heroic Christians died at Hitler's hand. It happens today in South and Central America and South Africa and elsewhere.

The church in El Salvador is deeply divided. Archbishop Oscar Romero was shot to death March 12, 1980, while saying mass. Many of the Catholic faithful—priests and

nuns and laypersons—have been killed by right-wing ter-
rorists—some with government blessing.

But the church is split between adherents of the
"theology of liberation" and those who are traditionally
supportive of those in power.

Some priests work actively with the opposition to the
government, giving credence to critics who accuse the
church of laying the groundwork for massive social
change through its teachings at the Jesuit-run university
and by organizational work among the poor.

But other priests serve as chaplains of government
military units. They denounce resistance and dispute the
belief that Romero, in the last month of his life, gave his
blessing to those working for dramatic changes in their
country.[15]

Consider in South Africa a Christian named Beyers
Naude. Born an Afrikaner, he was an ordained minister of
the Dutch Reformed Church in South Africa, and member
of the secret *Brooderbond*, or brotherhood, sworn to uphold white supremacy in South Africa. He became
chaplain of prestigious Pretoria University, and was
honored by being elected the Moderator of the Transvaal
Synod. Highly respected in government, church, and
educational circles, young Dr. Naude had a brilliant career
waiting for him.

But Beyers Naude had the gospel of Jesus working on
his mind and spirit. He became increasingly convinced
that apartheid (separation of the races) was contrary to
his Christian faith. He began to challenge the harsh,
restrictive policies directed toward black people. In
December 1960, then 45 years old, he spoke out firmly
against his government's racial policies at a meeting of
the World Council of Churches in Johannesburg. Naude's
own synod demanded he retract his statements and
confess his "error." He refused.

Since 1961, Beyers Naude's life was made increasingly
miserable. His status as a pastor was "withdrawn." He was

no longer allowed to preach a sermon in a Dutch Reformed Church. His friends fell away. His wife and children were harassed and threatened. His pension was canceled and his salary dropped.

In 1963, Naude tried to organize a Christian Institute to foster black-white dialogue and encourage black initiative. His church accused anyone associating with the Institute of "heresy." In 1977, the South African government "banned" the Institute and placed Naude under house arrest. He was not allowed to meet with more than one person at a time, to publish anything, to visit any educational institution, or to set foot in any African, colored, or Asian area.[16]

In the 1986 Philippine elections, when President Ferdinand Marcos was challenged by Corazon Aquino, the Roman Catholic Church was a prime organizational force behind the National Movement for Free Elections, a citizens' watchdog group that enlisted 500,000 volunteers. In nearly all 73 Philippine provinces, the bishops and local priests and nuns established the movement's teams in their areas.[17]

Marcos himself was a convert to Catholicism from his native Aglipayan religion. He was persuaded to join by his wife, Imelda, before they were married. Imelda visited the Manila compound where 110 bishops of the Philippines were sequestered. She sought to discourage them from making any statement on elections which seemed fraught with fraud by the ruling party. In spite of this, the bishops issued an unprecedented call for "nonviolent struggle" against the government for elections which the prelates called "unparalleled in ... fraudulence." Such a government, declared the bishops, "has no moral basis."[18]

How can members of the body of Christ be engaged in bringing poverty and pain to millions—sometimes in the name of Christ—while other Christians engage in a painful witness against that very injustice? Perhaps we suffer from amnesia, forgetting who we are and whose we are. Or maybe we never learned the simple, basic lessons in the first place. Maybe we were drawn into the institution without ever seeing the face of Christ himself, without ever having life turned around and made new. It happens.

"Growth" Under Fire

Not only is the church justifiably under fire. The very idea of growth is also under fire, especially as related to such an imperfect institution.

Many instinctively react against Church Growth today because of bad memories, or at least bad impressions of evangelism. "Evangelism" among many caring Christians in our day has a bad name.

Part of the problem is the success of non-Christians in using mass media to make all attempts to share the gospel seem cheap, crude, self-serving, and offensive.

I recall as a youth seeing the movie *Hawaii* in which missionaries were made to look foolish. Those idyllic islands were shown as a simple primitive paradise where people came together in love and trust to live out near-perfect lives. But the missionary, according to the movie, came with stern face and high-pitched tones to preach hell and judgment and to divide the people and forever destroy the beauty of primeval relationships there.

Later I read a response in a Christian youth magazine saying that the movie version was not true at all. The islands had indeed seemed a paradise. But the spoilers were not the missionaries but the sailors who came. They brought venereal disease and alcohol and selfishness and the worst of Western ways. And the paradise was forever shattered.

Then came the missionaries. The first missionaries who came were Congregationalists who preached not hate and judgment, but the *love* of God and the promise of a better life. They brought medicines and education and reintroduced the fellowship of love to a people who had lost it. They offered a way out of the hellish torment which earlier Westerners had introduced.[19]

Mass media (sometimes with justification) has painted efforts to share the gospel as bad. The movie image of the evangelist is often negative. So has been the movie image of the pastor, of dedicated Christians, and of the church itself. A feeling of shame has lingered in our minds. Even though we may find Christ and the church personally satisfying and helpful, we're not about to imitate the peddlers of religion who are heavy-handed, a little crooked, too impassioned, a little kooky, and often not to be trusted sexually.

So we cherish our faith deep in our hearts and never share it with a soul except maybe some good friend with whom we have near complete trust. And then maybe only superficially.

The Criticisms Are the Reason

But the very *truth* of the criticisms are the very reasons why sincere, dedicated Christians who have caught the vision *must* be about church growth. They must remember who they are. They are the ones who have dedicated themselves in the disciple Peter's words, "to follow in his steps" (1 Peter 2:21).

If we have a vision of what God really wants and are quiet, woe to us. We of all people must be about the task of sharing it.

And if we know what a powerful tool God intends his church to be and we see that tool misused, allowed to grow dull, and neglected, we of all people must dedicate ourselves to reclaim that tool. We must take it in from the mud and rain, clean it up, remove the rust, sharpen it again, and put it to the use which Christ intended.

No other institution on the earth will fulfill the task. The church alone is God's primary instrument to achieve his will. Of all human institutions, it alone is dedicated to bringing people into a living relationship with their Creator, Redeemer, Friend, and ultimate hope.

Jesus Lite

For many people, evangelism is a dirty word not simply because it has had a bad *press*, but because it has at times been *bad news*. Too easily the eternal news of God has been packaged to meet the tastes of men and women immersed in the affairs of this world without calling for change.

For the Mindanao tribesmen of the Philippines, the Christian settler's submachine guns speak instant news: no room for primitives. For the black Zulu, white Christian apartheid is neither good nor news. For many Indo-Chinese, the news of a Western Christ comes through as distinctly bad. How does an all-white gospel come through to the Chicano or the black?[1]

In college I sang in the a capella choir. We used to travel weekends to various churches to sing. Over Easter vacation we took a 10-day tour.

I recall returning to campus one rainy night. Driving the car was a black member of the choir, Wes, from a Roman Catholic home. A well-known evangelist came on the radio. Wes made no move to change the station. As he drove, we all listened.

Suddenly the car in front of us came to a complete stop. On the wet pavement, Wes's car slid, bumping into it. Wes got out. The driver ahead got out. But when he saw that Wes was black, he began a torrent of hateful words, many of them reflecting on Wes's blackness, on the character of his mother, and on things both religious and sexual in nature.

Wes did not argue back. He stood in the rain and took it. He gave the man his license number and the name of his insurance company. Then he got back in the car. We continued our long drive home, listening to the evangelist.

When the evangelist had finished, Wes turned off the radio and said quietly, "The trouble with people like that is that all you need to do is 'come to Jesus.' It doesn't matter how you treat people like me."

That was all. Not another word. And not a word from us. We all sat silent. In my mind were images, flashbacks of incidents on our trips. Good church people took us into their homes at night and fed us sumptuously at their potluck suppers. One by one some of them would come around and inquire, "That colored boy—does he date white girls?" Or, "When you are assigned to sleep somewhere, does he have his own bed or does one of you share a bed with him?"

My own anger grew to join whatever anger or despair Wes felt. I knew that the message of evangelism on the radio that night was not good but bad news for Wes. And therefore it was bad news to me, too.

God's Counselor at Work

Actually, that evangelist was Billy Graham. Later I was to learn that Graham had not done all that badly. He was from the South and served a Southern-based church. But he had been quite bold. I began to notice in the papers from time to time that he refused to preach unless auditoriums were open to all. He integrated his team. He spoke with increasing clarity during difficult times.

In later years, Billy Graham increasingly moved away from any hint of "Jesus Lite." His sermonic offerings became increasingly thoughtful, direct, and downright prophetic.

In a *Washington Post* interview he separated himself from the Moral Majority with the soul-searching comment, "You don't hear much (from them) about the hungry masses, the inner-city ghettos or the nuclear arms race."[2]

He opened himself to change because of close Christian friends, because the Scriptures taught him things he hadn't seen before, and because an awareness of the danger of our times added a new dimension. "I'd never thought it through before," he said in his support of the idea of "Salt 10"—the destruction of all nuclear weapons and biochemical weapons. "We have the ability to destroy the whole world.... We're spending $550 billion on nuclear arms around the world. It's already costing millions of lives because of the millions who are living on the knife edge of starvation."

God does work in the lives of his people. All of us begin where we are. But if our lives are open, the God who loves us does take us from where we are in the direction of what he wants us to become.

But some of us fear that may never happen.

I have a pastor friend who likes to use the Zenith phrase, "The quality goes in before the name goes on." He doesn't want to simply paste on a new name if the insides are as cheap and junky as before. His fear is not without justification.

Too recent in our memory are the Christians' support of slave trade. The first slave ship to land in Jamestown in 1619 was named *Jesus.* John Newton, captain of one of the slave ships, oversaw black cargo. They were chained together, not able to walk around, lying in their own excretion. A ceiling only a few feet from the floor permitted packing more in.

This captain watched the blacks suffer in the sweltering heat, knowing that some would die, knowing that they would be sold like cattle. Families would be deliberately broken up, women would be used for the sexual pleasure of white owners, and those who were weak or unfit would be discarded. That he could profit from such a sorry trade and yet write such lovely hymns as "How Sweet the Name of Jesus Sounds" or "Glorious Things of Thee are Spoken"[3] seems so perverse as to be obscene.

How can we know that the task will ever be completed? How can we know that the "Simon Peter" will ever get beyond the blustery, impulsive, loud-talking stage and settle into the "Rock" which God intends?

How can we know that the newborn who talks with such affection about Jesus with her lips and then makes a liar of herself by the way she lives will ever grow up to glorify in her life the name she wears? How can we be sure that if the name goes on, the quality will ever go in?

We don't. We don't know any more than a cynical onlooker in Jesus' day. Judas had betrayed him and Peter had denied him. All the other men close to him had fallen back into the shadows and shuddered in fear. Could such an onlooker believe that Jesus' investment and his trust in that unlikely crew would pay off?

Can a farmer know that seeds planted and watered and tended do indeed grow into plants and one day yield grain? Can a parent be certain that children in a home—loved, disciplined, taught, mothered and fathered, fed and clothed and watched over, cried and worried over—one day will make their parents proud? We simply don't know.

One Step at a Time

One of the keys to church growth, according to Donald McGavran, father of the modern Church Growth movement, is the ability of those who would share the gospel to distinguish between what McGavran called "discipling" and what he called "perfecting." We have to be willing to start with people *where they are*—at their recognized point of need. Start with where they hurt. Accept them, love them, nurture and guide them, and let them grow into what God wants.[4]

It never happens in one giant bite. Healthy Christians are not like some teenage boys I know very well who can proudly down a Big Mac in two bites and, by the sweep second hand on their watches, do it all in six seconds.

That may be a good attention-getter. But that is not the way healthy growth takes place.

"WHAT?... You mean No ONE brought the buns?"

I have a 64-year-old friend who is trim and lean. He is in better shape than he was 25 years ago. Long ago his mother instructed him to chew each bite 32 times. And he has. And he does.

That may be way too much for most of us. But somewhere between two bites for one burger and 32 chews for a small spoonful of peas, there must be a happier medium.

The focus must be clear. Elton Trueblood put it simply: "A Christian is a person who confesses that, amidst the manifold and confusing voices heard in the world, there is one Voice which supremely wins his full assent, uniting all his powers, intellectual and emotional, into a single pattern of self-giving. That Voice is Jesus Christ."[5]

But with the apostle Paul we must confess and affirm: "Not that I have already obtained this or am already perfect; but I press on to make it my own. . . . Brethren, I do not consider that I have made it my own; but one thing I do, forgetting what lies behind and straining forward to what lies ahead, I press on toward the goal for the prize of the upward call of God in Christ Jesus" (Philippians 3:12-14, RSV).

Karl Barth puts it somewhat differently. He writes of "*a clear decision* against the old man and the old form of the world which can only disappear now that they have been set aside. The community of Jesus Christ sees this decision taken in him. It keeps to it. It follows it. It follows it in world-occurrence and therefore within the limits of its own possibilities. Yet it does follow it, not as an idle spectator, but *in active obedience*. It follows, *not in one great absolute step, but in several small and relative steps. But it really does follow it.*"[6]

Jesus gave the good news to his followers bite-size, one step at a time. They grew . . . slowly, sometimes fitfully. Sometimes they took one step forward and two back. But they did grow, some of them, just as Jesus himself grew "in wisdom and in stature, and in favor with God and man" (Luke 2:52, RSV).

A God Who Is Still at Work

I'm amazed at how God works his wondrous will in mysterious ways among us. About when I'm ready to give up and write off some group which names his name as unfit to be a part of his army, they amaze me by opening up to him in a way I never would have imagined.

How strong has been the prejudice among many Protestants toward Roman Catholics! Oceans of history and theology and misunderstanding have separated us. Surely the Catholics had ulterior plans, we felt.

I recall newspaper ads about evangelists lecturing on "the Beast" when I was a child in Lima, Ohio. At first the Beast was "proven" to be Hitler. Then, with Hitler gone, it was Stalin. Then Mao. And then the pope. Catholics were surely the children of the antichrist—God's enemy on earth.

Then along came Pope John XXIII, the man who was to be a breather, an interim between popes. And what a joyous surprise he was as he threw open the windows. "All I want to do," he said, "is to let in a little fresh air." And Catholics opened the Scriptures in a way that embarrassed many Protestants. And they began to move the furniture around in their staid church. And they proved they had more courage to change than any had dreamed possible. God is at work among them. It should be obvious to all the world.

Locally, we see pastors who couldn't talk to each other a few years back. Now they come together regularly to break bread and share understandings. Holiness and SDAs and "mainliners" actually talk like brothers and sisters with the same Lord and Savior. Suddenly truths which we thought were exclusively ours we find springing up in the strangest ground. We see services of healing among the Episcopalians. Social concern among evangelicals. Evangelism among the mainline respectable middle and upper class.

I once sat in a class at Fuller with perhaps a half-dozen

members of the Seventh-Day Adventist Church. One of them talked with tears in his eyes of the joy of being able for the first time to know fellowship with others who loved and served Jesus. In that class were Pentecostals, Church of Christ, Episcopal, "mainline" clergy and executives.

Mormon theology is worlds removed from my own. Some argue effectively that the Church of Jesus Christ of Latter-Day Saints is not Christian. Dave Hunt and Ed Decker, a former Mormon, in their explosive book, *The God Makers,* contend that Mormonism is closer to Hinduism than to Christianity.[7] But one of the things that frightened me most was their *application* of their theology. I loved their great Mormon Tabernacle Choir, but I feared their attitudes, especially toward other races. How might America be affected as they grow in numbers and influence?

Then a secular newspaper, the *Los Angeles Times,* gave me a whole new perspective of the devious and marvelous way in which our God can work among those we consider unlikely people, sneaking in at a point where they least expect it.

Basketball is a part of Mormon life. It almost seems as essential as their family nights and their abstinence from alcohol, coffee, and tea.

Something happened in the very center of Mormonism to shatter the walls of race separation. A professional basketball team from New Orleans—the Jazz—moved to Salt Lake City and became the "Utah Jazz" (a strange title for that location). Into that devout setting where basketball is a part of their community life, great black players came to walk their streets, eat in their restaurants, live next door, and win their hearts on the hardwood. An unlikely romance was established. And God, mysterious, mischievous, and very subtle was opening doors.[8]

The Mormons have not been exactly one of the historic peace churches. But someone in the defense establishment committed a grave tactical error when he decided to deploy an MX missile system across the Southwest in the very areas where Mormons are most in abundance. The proposal suddenly made Mormon homes and farms potential targets in any future nuclear war.

Hiroshima made many Japanese passionate spokespersons for peace. Every soldier I have ever talked to who went through the Battle of the Bulge said, "Never again." General Sherman said, "I am tired and sick of war. Its glory is all moonshine. It is only those who have neither fired a shot, nor heard the shrieks and groans of the wounded, who cry aloud for blood, more vengeance, more desolation. War is hell."

In the same way, Spencer Kimball, at that time the president of the Mormon Church, deplored in a Christmas message to all church members "the unrestricted building of arsenals of war, including huge and threatening nuclear weaponry." While acknowledging that "America must be strong," he called upon all people to "save the world from a holocaust, the depth and breadth of which can scarcely be imagined."[9]

Someone higher up in defense planning goofed when he openly called Utah and Nevada the ideal "aim point" or "sponge" for absorbing a nuclear attack. He may have begun a sensitizing process among an entire faith group. The ultimate impact on the life of our nation and the world is absolutely mind-boggling.

But it gets much simpler than that. It happens in your life and mine. Just about the time one of us gets self-righteous and proud, some tragedy strikes. We can lash out against sinners in a most un-Christlike manner, and sin visits us where it hurts the most. God keeps visiting us, calling us, chastising us, shamelessly exposing us, leading us.

I heard a former evangelist confess, "I was filled with hate. Hatred for sinners. Hatred for liars and thieves and adulterers and perverts and cheats. Then my own home fell apart and I realized just how full of hate I was. The love of God was not in me. My wife could not live with me. Nor my children. I realized I didn't even want to live with myself anymore the way I was."

Jesus could be very hard on people—on self-righteous people, on proud religious, legalistic snobs. But on the hurting, the lost, those caught in the web of sin, he could be very gentle, very encouraging, very kind, very forgiving. He could love people without loving what they did.

How can anyone do that? the cynic will ask. Aren't people really what they do?

One day I heard someone say, "There is one person toward whom I have been doing that all her life—accepting her without accepting all that she does."

"Who is that?" I asked.

"Myself," she replied.

Most of us tend to accept ourselves, even though we know in our hearts (in our more honest moments) that some of what we do is downright rotten.

And all Jesus asks is that we do for our brothers and sisters what we do for ourselves. "Do for others just what you want them to do for you" (Luke 6:31, TEV).

Never minimize the message of the Christ. Never compromise the cost. Keep crystal clear who he is and what he wants. *Jesus Lite* will never quench the deep thirst of hurting humanity. Come to hurting people gently, with love.

That's all that God wants. And that is one of the keys which Church Growth has discovered. Begin where people *are*, with their hopes, their fears, their hurts, their felt needs. That must be the starting point.

Newton Revisited

We used John Newton, the slave trader who also authored hymns, as an example of what ought not to be. Actually, his story is an example of what can happen through the power of God.

Newton's father had been a ship's captain and sailed

the Mediterranean ports.[10] John never saw his father until he was seven years old. His mother was his constant companion. She was a devout member of the Church of England and saw to it that John attended church, prayed, and read the Bible.

When she died, there was no place for John to go except to his father's fishing ship. From the age of eight he lived amid the swearing, drinking, and wild talk and life of his father's ships.

At the age of 17, he was seized for service on a British man-o'-war but escaped and signed up on a ship in the slave trade. He soon was known as the "best blasphemer" on all British boats. He could talk so foul and swear so loud. He was a drunk, a murderer, and a totally immoral sailor.

In Africa he became so drunk that he missed his boat and for a number of years was the slave of an African woman who, glorying in her power over him, made him depend for his food on the crusts that she tossed under her table.

A Portuguese slave ship rescued him and hired him in the slave trade to Charleston, South Carolina. Off Newfoundland, in 1748, a violent storm hit the ship and all hands gave it up for lost. Now 23 years of age, Newton remembered a sentence from his mother's prayers. "Lord, have mercy upon us." He cried out to God for help and, as he puts it, "The Lord came from on high and delivered me out of deep waters."

When the storm-battered ship finally arrived in Ireland, Newton did not forget the mercy of God. He was a changed person. He quit the sea and prepared for ministry in the Church of England.

He served for ten years as rector in St. Mary's Woolnuth. In his congregation was a man named Wilberforce. It is no accident that this man accepted the leadership of the forces that abolished slavery in the British Empire.

Newton wrote the following hymn:

> Amazing grace! how sweet the sound.
> That saved a wretch like me!
> I once was lost, but now am found.
> Was blind but now I see.

That hymn takes on a whole new meaning when we see it as a statement of Newton's own life.

Newton goes on:

> Twas grace that taught my heart to fear.
> And grace my fears relieved.
> How precious did that grace appear
> The hour I first believed.

Near the end of his life, Newton met William Jay on the streets of London. As they exchanged Christian greetings, Newton said to his friend, "My memory is gone. But I remember two things: I am a great sinner. And Jesus Christ is my Savior." On his memorial stone are the words:

> JOHN NEWTON
> Clerk.
> Once an infidel and libertine,
> A Servant of Slaves in Africa
> was by the Mercy of our Lord and Savior
> Jesus Christ
> Preserved, restored, pardoned,
> And appointed to preach the faith
> he had so long
> laboured to destroy.

Some critics of Church Growth say it does not place enough trust in the Holy Spirit. But in the most important principle of beginning where people are, it manifests tremendous trust in the Holy Spirit.

Jesus told his followers: "I have much more to tell you, but now it would be too much for you to bear. When, however, the Spirit comes, who reveals the truth about God, he will lead you into all the truth" (John 16:12-13, TEV). Believing that is essential to some of the basic assumptions of Church Growth.

Jesus' Peter Principle

When did Peter become a disciple? Was it when, along the shores of the lake, he heard the call of Christ, "Come, follow me"? Was it when he dropped his nets and turned his back on his former life—his boats, his friends, his wife, his job—and went with Jesus? (Matthew 4:18-20). Or was it later, when Jesus had them alone and asked, "Who do men say that [I am]?" and the disciples offered various answers: "Elijah." "Moses." "One of the prophets." But Jesus pressed them. "But who do *you* say that I am?" The impulsive Peter, so eager and so ready to talk, burst forth with, "You are the Christ, the Son of the living God" (Matthew 16:13-16, RSV). Was he a disciple then?

Or was it when Jesus invited him to walk to him across the water and Peter suddenly realized how little faith he had? (Matthew 14:25-31). Or was it when he was asleep in the boat and was awakened by the storm that Peter realized his need and his helplessness? (Matthew 8:23-26).

Or was it in the garden when Peter was so ready to defend his Lord? Then he received the lesson, "Put your sword back.... All who take the sword will perish by the sword" (Matthew 26:52, RSV).

Was Peter a disciple when he stood back in the shadows while Jesus was on trial? He did not sound like a disciple when a little slave girl said, "You are one of them. Your hillbilly talk gave you away." When he began to swear and insist he did not know the man—was he a disciple then? (Matthew 26:69-75).

On Easter Sunday morning, when Peter greeted the risen Christ—was that the moment that he became a disciple? (John 21:15-19). Or was it in Jerusalem as they waited together and prayed together and received the Holy Spirit—was that the moment it began? (Acts 1:12-15). Or was it much, much later, when Peter confronted his own racism with the visit of the servant of Cornelius and came to realize that indeed God shows no partiality but in every nation those who fear him are acceptable to him? that those of us who are not Jewish are not unclean and not forever unacceptable before God? (Acts 10).

When did Peter become a disciple? At what point?

What about you and me? When are *we* truly disciples?

I recall some years ago viewing the very moving Billy Graham film, "A Time to Run." It was the heart-rending story of a young man and his family who were running away from themselves and from God. In the end they "come to themselves," to use the biblical phrase (Luke 15:17).

Our 76-year-old minister of visitation at the time, Roy Forney, listened as I babbled on about what I thought of the movie. Suddenly I thought to ask Roy what he thought. His comment was a single sentence. He said, "It stopped where it should have started."

For many Christians—both those who talk much about being "born again" and those who want a great deal of ethical content—it's all over when it begins. The Christian faith is one giant leap, one big bite—all or nothing. But God doesn't work that way.

In the college church I served was a former president of the college who was a former English professor and an ordained minister, Ralph Schlosser—deeply loved and respected. That 86-year-young man was baptizing a 70-some-year-old man of Pennsylvania Dutch background.

When the immersion was completed, the man looked up from the baptismal waters into Schlosser's face and, in German, the new Christian said, "Thank God, it's over now." But Ralph Schlosser replied in German, "No, my friend, it is just beginning."

God would take you and me on a journey. Every journey must have a beginning. This journey takes us over roads we never traveled before. At each turn of the road, we discover things we did not even know were there. We do not see the end. But we begin. We follow. And we keep discovering. And for the Christian, that journey never ends.

Augustine said of the Christian experience, "Perfect pilgrims, not yet perfect possessors."

Sets—Bounded, Centered, or Fuzzy

Helpful to my understanding has been the thought of Paul Hiebert of the School of World Mission at Fuller Theological Seminary. As a cultural anthropologist, Hiebert points out that various peoples use different processes to form their categories.[1]

We of the West tend to look upon life in terms of *bounded sets.* An onion is always an onion. Onions may be thin, spring onions, or fat Bermudas. They may be green or white or yellow or red. But everyone knows an onion. An onion is never an apple.

When we look at life, we Westerners tend to see clear boundaries. The objects around us have distinct characteristics. The categories are static, unchanging.

We tend to be this way in our patriotism. "America: Love it or Leave it" is a familiar bumper sticker. Either you are or you are not one hundred percent American. There is no middle ground. Those who say they criticize their country (or their town or their school or their conditions at work) because they love it, never quite make sense to many people.

Many Christians see *Christians* as a bounded set. Ask them, "What is a Christian?" Some may define it in terms

BOUNDED SET   CENTERED SET

of a creed. Fundamentalists will list what for them are the
defining fundamentals. Before World War I a couple of
businessmen were concerned about the newly popular
theory of evolution and they set forth in some pamphlets
what they believed to be the essentials for being a Christian under the title "The Fundamentals of the Christian
Faith." They listed the inerrancy of the Scriptures in every
detail, the Virgin Birth, the Substitutionary Theory of the
atonement, the physical resurrection of Christ, the personal and visible return of Christ, and the physical resurrection of the dead.

But others, not wanting to be called Fundamentalists,
also would define the faith in terms of a creed or faith
statement. With what vigor Christians have fought over
creeds! They would argue that there are clearly defined
beliefs which everyone who is a Christian will hold—a
bounded set.

Still others see Christianity as an ethical code. "How
can a person be a Christian and do such a thing?"

From this perspective, evangelism is getting people to cross over the boundary into the circle of the elect (or "faithful").

But there is another way of defining things. Some see things more in terms of *centered sets,* says Hiebert. Here the defining characteristic is not the *boundary* one draws but rather *what is the center?* There may be a clear boundary but there is a degree of variation. This is illustrated by a magnetic force—a positive pole which attracts some elements and repels others. Centered sets are dynamic sets. There is always movement—either (1) change of direction, or (2) movement toward or away from the center.

Rather than asking, "Are you healthy?" as if health were an absolute, we understand that each of us is moving toward or away from health. Nothing is ever static.

To see Christians in terms of a centered set is to realize that the critical question is not whether a person is *in* or *out* but, rather, "Where are you going in relation to the center?" Is your face or your back toward Christ? Are you moving toward him or away?

There is a clear division, but maintenance of lines and boundaries is less critical than asking, "Who is Lord?" There is a recognition of variations. Conversion is "to turn around" not to "cross over the line."

Some may be very far from Christ, like the woman at the well (John 4:5-42). Or the woman caught in adultery (John 8:1-11). Or the tax collectors who sat at table with him (Luke 15:1-2). But they were moving toward him.

Others may be very close. No group in Jesus' day was closer to Jesus than the Pharisees. Their theology and outlook were very similar. But they were moving away from him even though in many ways they seemed closer than the lost and the least who loved him so.

How many times I have seen saints of the church, longtime members, born into the church, recipients of the third or fourth generation of faith, nevertheless grown

satisfied, smug, cold, and indifferent, having lost the vision of his love and his life. In the midst of the fellowship
will be a newborn babe—maybe old in years but fresh and
young in commitment—so eager, so hungry, so dedicated.
In terms of the centered set concept, the question is not
where are you on some graph, but what direction are you
moving?

There is, says Paul Hiebert, a *third* way of forming categories. Egyptian mathematicians—and more recently,
Japanese mathematicians—have talked of *fuzzy sets.*

We of the West tend to think of people being Christians
or not. Many Orientals see all religions blending. (There
are many roads up the mountain.) They ask, why not a
Hindu *and* a Christian?

Music of India lacks the clear definition we know. It
seems to run together and take liberties which leave us
feeling jumpy. Roads in southern California are clearly
marked. There are fast lanes, slow lanes, and truck lanes.
There are diamond lanes for cars with two or more
passengers. There are bike lanes in some areas. There are
clear definitions of where pedestrians walk and do not
walk. But in India the road blends into the countryside. An
Oriental will ask, "Where does the mountain begin?"

There is a story about a famous racist governor of a
deep South state. The physician had finished his exami-
nation. "I have good news and bad news," the doctor said.

"Let's have the good news first," said the governor.

"All right. The good news is that you have six months to
live."

"That's the good news? What is the bad news?"

"The bad news is that you have sickle-cell anemia."

When is a black a black? If all ancestors are black? But
what if one of four grandparents is white? What if two
were white? What if three were white? When is a black?

With bounded sets, an object is in or out. With fuzzy
sets, one may run into another.

Paul Hiebert said sadly, "Sometimes as I look at my congregation I see it as a fuzzy set." It lacks a clear sense of what it is about. It blends too easily into the world.

Fear of the Fuzzy

John Howard Yoder, questioning the principle of discipling and perfecting, wondered about "superficial loyalty." He asked, "What is minimal (to becoming a Christian) and what is dispensable supplement? If not everything belongs to the minimum, what does?"[2]

He offered examples where a society has patterns sharply at odds with Christian understandings.

> One of the questions here is the logic of nurture: If we have said by our silences that an issue is not important as a part of the meaning of membership, on what grounds will we explain its importance later? Especially this becomes a problem with regard to visible social issues.
>
> If we have not said the Christian church is an integrated community at the point of winning people to membership initially, what authority will we have to call for a movement toward integration later? ... Here I am not arguing the issue of racial integration as related to the definition of the church ... but only asking by what principles we can interpret the distinction between what is minimal and what is not.[3]

Yoder effectively pressed to know what church growth people felt is basic to becoming a Christian.

> Is there some concept of what might be called moral "curriculum," that always distinguishes between what you learn first and what you learn later?
>
> Is there some assumption about what constitutes saving faith which determines the threshold? Is there some scale of moral priority issues, some of which are indispensable and others dispensable?[4]

Offering two striking examples of Christian communities located in, first, an oppressive racist culture and,

second, in a land of oppressive militarism, Yoder asked, "Do you win people by withholding part of the gospel from those who come?. . . Can the *content of nurture* ever really contradict the *message of evangelism?*"[5]

Yoder offers a troubling example.

Latin American civilization is the result of powerfully effective church growth. Catholicism was able to take over the continent by baptizing all the pagans and then did not get around to nurturing them. That opened up the phenomenon of syncretism in which spiritism or snake worship or sun worship could all be swept into Christian cultic practice.[6]

What Yoder has described so well is a fuzzy set concept. A Christianity which blends indistinguishably into the adjacent countryside. An undefined, purposeless blob.

Seeing Our Faith as a Centered Set

My own feeling is that the centered set concept fits most directly the Jesus way of working with people. It is helpful in several ways.

First, *it allows for a strong understanding of what it means to be a Christian.* It allows for the *costly grace* concept advanced by Bonhoeffer.

In his book, *The Cost of Discipleship,* Bonhoeffer argues that Christianity is not essentially a set of beliefs nor is it first of all a set of moral or ethical principles. Bonhoeffer wrote, "The call goes forth, and is at once followed by the response of obedience. The response of the disciples is an act of obedience, not a confession of faith in Jesus."[7]

As Jesus walked by the tax office and summoned Levi to follow him, as he called Simon Peter to leave his nets, in the same manner, he calls us.

"Because Jesus is the Christ, he has the authority to call and to demand obedience to his word. Jesus summons men to follow him not as a teacher or a pattern of the good life, but as the Christ, the Son of God."[8]

We are to go not knowing what it means or where he will take us.

Follow me, run along behind me! That is all. To follow in his steps is something which is void of all content. . . . The disciple simply *burns his boats* and goes ahead. He is called out, and has to forsake his old life.... It is nothing else than bondage to Jesus Christ alone, completely breaking through every programme, every ideal, every set of laws.... He alone matters.[9]

Second, the centered set concept *makes possible meeting persons where they are.*

It focuses on people and their need and on Christ rather than on where to draw lines. It is reflected in the Gospels at many points. One example is Jesus' response to the woman caught in the act of adultery (John 8:1-11). Another is Jesus' response to the Sabbath laws (Luke 6:1-11).

Ray Anderson wrote:

When evangelical faith adopts a "boundary mentality," it becomes fundamentalist.... When fundamentalism and liberalism attack each other in the name of the truth of God, the struggle is over *where* the boundaries are to be drawn. The true antithesis, on the other hand, is between the historical transcendence of God and *all* boundaries which seek to contain God or identify God through the laws of creaturehood, whether they are defined in religious, ethical or rational terms.[10]

Jesus was more concerned about people than boundaries. As he approached each individual, he was like a boat sailing around an island until he arrived at the place to embark.

To a rich young ruler he said, "Go and sell all that you have and give the money to the poor" (Mark 10:20, *The Living Bible).* But from a corrupt tax collector he welcomed the commitment, "Sir, from now on I will give half my wealth to the poor" (and what was even more important for Zacchaeus) "and if I have overcharged anyone on his taxes, I will penalize myself by giving him back four times as much" (Luke 19:8, LB).

Peter Wagner talks of being "receptor-oriented," of beginning at the point of each person's felt need or guilt.[11]

He says, "At baptism I was a drunkard. That was my point of guilt. I wasn't concerned about racism or oppression in Latin America or abortion."

Wagner tells of Dwight L. Moody giving an invitation. Later, a well-dressed woman came to Moody and said, "If I become a Christian, is it necessary for me to walk down the aisle?"

Moody's reply was, *"Now* it is." Five minutes ago it would not have been, but she made it an issue.

Third, *the centered set concept saves us from having to dump the whole load at once.*

The apostle Paul knew that babies in the faith are not ready for meat. They begin with milk (1 Cor. 3:2).

Years ago, Art Linkletter interviewed a child psychologist on the question of sex education for children. The psychologist's advice applies here. He advised that children (1) always be told the truth. As you talk about sex, never say anything that will have to be unlearned later. His next point was, (2) Do not go beyond what a child is ready to receive. A youngster asked her mother, "Mommy, where did I come from?" The mother brought out charts and pictures and gave a minor course in biology. The child sat through it patiently and then asked her question again. "What I want to know is, did we come from Ohio or Indiana?" Answer the child's questions openly and honestly, but only as the child is ready to receive what needs to be learned.

The same applies in the Christian faith. I asked Peter Wagner what he would say if a Klansman came to him and inquired about his faith. Wagner replied, "If he came saying his home was breaking up and he needed help, I would begin at that point." If we would win others to Christ we must begin *at the point of their need.* We must even be willing to take a step back, if need be, as the apostle Paul implied when he said, "To the Jews I became as a Jew [again] . . . I have become all things to all men, that I might by all means save some" (1 Corinthians 9:20, 22, RSV).

Trusting God to Work His Will

Finally, *this concept allows us to trust God to work his will in the lives of his children.*

Earlier we noted that Jesus said to his disciples, "There is so much more I want to tell you, but you can't understand it now" (John 16:12, LB).

There were so many things he wanted to share but they were not yet ready. But he added a promise: "When the Holy Spirit, who is truth, comes, he shall guide you into all truth" (John 16:13, LB).

> The dictionary definition of "disciple" helps: "dis-ci-ple n. 1. a pupil or follower . . ."[12]

Orlando Costas said it well: "To become a disciple of Christ is to enter into a learning relationship with him, a process that never ends." But, as he also notes, "The beginning of this relationship is not without its demands."[13]

Baptism is not a "last rite" but a point of entrance. To be a disciple by definition is to be a *learner,* not to have graduated.

Donald McGavran drew heavily on the studies of a Methodist bishop, J. Wanscom Pickett, who insisted that it really did not matter how a person found entrance into the church. Some came for social reasons; friends or family were coming. Some for selfish reasons. They want a better job, more social standing. Some came out of curiosity. Some out of genuine dedication.

But across the years the reasons for entrance became almost indistinguishable. What mattered far more than why they came was the quality of nurture provided. If the nurture was good, Christians matured. If there was no nurture, if the feeding and care of newborn Christians was inadequate, the results were poor, too.[14]

I think of a lad who was a member of the Lancaster, Pennsylvania, Church of the Brethren. He wanted to be a Green Beret. But when the officers discovered his background was Church of the Brethren, a historic peace church, his request was denied.

"But," he protested, "I am not a pacifist. I reject that part of my religious background."

"Despite what you say," they informed him, "we know from past experience that because of your background there will come a time when you will be given an order and you will refuse to follow it. We cannot afford for that to happen."

The boy protested vigorously, but to no avail. He went into the regular army. But at one point while stationed in Germany, he was given an order and he and several friends refused to obey.

There is a conditioning that takes place in every church. "You can take the boy out of the Baptists but you cannot take the Baptist out of the boy," each group says, substituting its own name.

The key is not how they came in—whether by Caesarean or natural birth—but what they were fed and how they were nurtured once in.

So let us fear a little less and trust God a little more that he will indeed do in other lives—those not so far along the road as we—what he has done in us. And let us grant others the freedom, the patience, and the love to find their way into the fullness of his grace—the same freedom and patience and love that we hungered for, and insisted on, for ourselves.

Are We Trying to Program the Holy Spirit?

Bad memories and uneasiness about trusting God to continue to lead his people into his truth have soured some to Church Growth. Among others there is added resistance to Church Growth because of what seems to be secular dependence on what should be a purely *faith* operation. Some suspect that Church Growth principles are more sociological than religious, that proponents are taking a leaf from some college or university textbook rather than from the Scriptures.

Are we trying to program the Holy Spirit? Why not just let God do his work in his own time and his own way? If we are faithful, devout, and prayer-full, isn't that sufficient?[1]

Clearly the Scriptures say that faith sharing involves both God and us. Because I am not a grower of grapes I never really understood that agricultural reference of Jesus, "I am the vine, you are the branches ..." (John 15:5, RSV). It never occurred to me that *vines do not bear fruit.* Branches do—but only branches tied in a living way into the vine.

The other agricultural parables also escaped me. I had not thought deeply about what they were saying about soils, soil preparation, care, and harvesting. It took a former "Aggie," a student of agriculture turned missionary and Church Growth theoretician—Peter Wagner—to begin to open up to me what Jesus was saying about our part and God's part (Matthew 13:3-9). The clear message is that it doesn't "just happen." It takes the thought, planning, care, and persistence which every good farmer knows.

Evangelience

One day while shaving I reflected on the name of my wife's shampoo—Silkience. From the back of the bottle comes this wisdom:

> Your hair is different all over. It may be healthy near the scalp, weakened in the middle, or dry or damaged at the ends. That means that you have different conditioning requirements all over your hair. Now there is *Silkience* . . . formulated to adjust automatically to your various conditioning needs. It gives just the right amount . . . no more, no less. *Silkience:* "The science of silkening your hair."

My mind reflected: evangelscience . . . evangeliscience . . . evangelience. Is that what we are working at? Church Growth has discovered that every congregation is different. Unique patterns of Christian understanding call for individualized strategies and carefully tooled programs. Evangelism is so important to many Christians. Yet "evangelism" is not a word found in the New Testament. The New Testament speaks of the *evangel*—the good news. But evangel*ism* is *our* word.

I have a pastor friend who does research in the Philadelphia area for those who sell homes and cars. He asks, What kind of home sells? What kind of car sells? Often the car that brings the customer into the showroom is not the car that the customer buys. A red convertible would bring them in, he used to say. But few would ever *buy* a red convertible.

He asked the question, "When people use the word 'evangelism,' what do they mean?" Often they have in mind a mood, certain familiar words, or some gospel songs they associate with earlier memories. They may or may not have in mind sharing their faith, reaching out to bring non-Christians to Christ. Someone says "evangelism" and we think "Billy Graham." Or someone may say "evangelism" and we assume, "Oh, he wants me to go knock on doors."

Several years ago I went to an evangelism conference several hundred miles away. I went reluctantly. I went because I felt I ought to go. I went thinking I would hear someone talk about emotion and getting geared up psychologically to talk more about our faith. I expected to hear the usual evangelistic words: "saved" and "lost" and "blood" and "the cross."

Instead I heard a man—Win Arn—show a series of overheads and talk about scientific research. He said, among other things, that 70 to 80 percent of the people who come into a church do not come because of blind visitation or evangelistic crusades or the pastor or the church school. One thousandth of one percent come through crusades. But from 70 to 80 percent come because of some friend or relative![2]

Arn said the aim of evangelism is to lead people to "become disciples and responsible members of Christ's church." The task is not complete with a decision. Apart from the vine, a branch shrivels and dies. There must be a tie into the body of Christ. Otherwise, newborn Christians are like orphans abandoned on a doorstep. They have as great a chance of survival.

The usual pattern is to cast about and pick up others' good programs. Many who talk about evangelism concern themselves with methodology and program—like busing to church school, or offering prizes.

Win Arn was talking about helping each congregation understand its strengths, deepen its faith, and diagnose its "health." Each could be trained in those approaches which make for growth and then begin to develop, step by step, strategies that uniquely fit its situation and the gifts which God has given it. He was talking of a carefully tooled program, custom-built for each setting, like Silkience for distinctly differing needs in a single head of hair.

Evangelience. I've never heard the word used before. Maybe it will strike a negative chord in the hearts of some. At first glance it may appear that we are trying to reduce the Holy Spirit to our own human calculations.

More accurately, what we are struggling with is an approach different from whipping up enough emotion in our little hearts to do it all. As theology is the queen of the sciences, the attempt to think carefully, logically about God, so evangelology—evangelience—could be described as an attempt to use all that God has given us, to survey the need, to hear the cries of hurting and lost humanity.

To more fully understand our task. To evaluate what we have tried in the past. To see what things have not helped but hurt. To recognize that sometimes what we thought were our best efforts were in fact brilliant notions which misfired. To sort out the things that can best help us to achieve the immense, divine task to which God himself has called us. And then we can begin to use them!

In World War 2 as Allied troops overran former Nazi death camps, they discovered they did not know how to bring starving men and women back to health. They tried feeding them. But it felt like a new form of torture to them. How does one proceed? With IVs? Partially digested foods? How? In a similar fashion, how does one bring spiritually starving children of God from their famine to a life of wholeness and nourishment?

I attended Win Arn's weeklong Advanced Growth Seminar with the wide range of participants—from Episcopal priests to Salvation Army officers, from United Methodists and United Presbyterians to Holiness people, from Mennonites and Brethren to whatever. Language was a problem, but the concepts applied across the board. I was impressed and helped.

After my encounter with Win Arn, I went further. I decided to go to the center of the ferment of this new approach to sharing the evangel. I discovered that the "father" of this outlook was a former third-generation missionary for the Disciples of Christ, an 80-some-year-old man to whom we have already referred—Donald McGavran. In India he labored during one seven-year period without a single convert. He had asked the difficult questions, questions which his colleagues did not want to hear. Why do some churches grow while others do not? Why does the same denomination grow in one place but not another, or in one time but not another? Others said it was a matter of faith ... or of faithfulness. Because they preached the true gospel, they grew. Or because they dared to preach the true gospel, they lost members while others grew.[3]

But he found certain patterns worldwide. And began to collect data. Like Charles Darwin and his study of fruit flies, he carefully recorded it all. McGavran began to say there are keys to help us in carrying out the mandate of the great commission.[4]

One Unifying Factor

What do an evangelical like Peter Wagner and a "mainliner" United Methodist like George Hunter III have in common? What attracts an Anabaptist like myself to studies in a recognized conservative school like Fuller with a third-generation missionary out of the Disciples of Christ and an accused Calvinist like Arthur Glasser? What brings Pentecostals and United Presbyterians, charismatics and charismatic-resisting members of the Church of Christ together in number?

Charles Arn, artist and idea man for the Institute for American Church Growth, said in an offhand moment, "The unifying strand is a conviction that lost people must be found, that there are hurting, lonely, dying people around us and that Jesus Christ is the answer."

Donald McGavran: Task Theologian

It is important to say that as McGavran examined growing and declining churches around the world, the answers he found were not couched in theological terms. Every great event in biblical history preceded people's reflection in theological terms about what it meant. So is it in our own lives. Events happen to us and we respond. A child is born. A dear friend dies. We experience a dramatic change in our job. A relationship breaks down.

After each such event the thoughtful Christian reexamines what has happened and the response that was made in light of an eternal faith. Karl Barth says, "Every Christian as such is called to be a theologian."[5] There is truth in Ray Anderson's suggestion that "ministry precedes and produces theology." Out of ministry "emerges theological activity, exploring and expounding the nature and purpose of God in and for creation and human creatures."[6]

Donald McGavran was so involved in an emerging superstructure that he did not always provide the theological background some would have liked. Paul Hiebert of the Fuller School of World Mission has referred to McGavran as "a task theologian."

Mennonites and Episcopalians, Four Square Gospellers and Lutherans have been struck by the beauty, the simplicity, and the striking similarity to New Testament patterns. It is understandable that they should return to their own traditions and theology and seek to explain Church Growth discoveries in terms of their own experience, tying it into their own heroes, doctrine, and biblical understanding.

"Wrong Locus"

Orlando Costas charged the movement with a questionable theological "locus."[7]

He quoted Alan Tippett who said, "Church growth does not cover the whole range of Christian theology."[8]

"Instead," [citing Peter Wagner] "it has concentrated its efforts on ecclesiology," charged Costas. And "by so doing, it has made the church the 'locus' of its theological reflection. The outcome of this has been a theology of mission that revolves around the church instead of God's redemptive action in Christ [which is the basis for the existence of the church]."[9]

The result, according to Costas, is a church-centered theology that mitigates "against the 'locus' of biblical theology: Christ."[10]

To affirm that the aim of evangelism is the multiplication of churches is to advocate a theology that makes the church the end of God's mission.

> Isn't the gospel the good news of the *kingdom?* Who is the center of the kingdom—Christ or the church? Who is the object of the kingdom—the community or the King? What is the aim of the kingdom—the exercise of Christ's righteous, peaceful and loving reign in *heaven* and on *earth* in a restored and transformed universe, or the gathering of a community to him?

While conceding that the church is a "temporary goal," Costas wants to know if there is not much more to mission than church planting.

The answer must be, "Of course."

Karl Barth expresses it when he asserts,

> The community would be nothing if it did not come from the kingdom and go towards it; if the kingdom were not present in this transitional movement. . . . The kingdom of God grows like a seed. It is for this reason that the community also grows—the fellowship of men who with open eyes and ears and hearts come from Jesus Christ, from the kingdom of God, and move towards Him. It grows as it gives Him room to grow, and to the extent that it "decreases," as the Baptist said of himself. It lives because and as its Lord lives. It lives wholly and utterly as His people.[11]

At many points McGavran wrote movingly in his classic, *Understanding Church Growth.*

> As in the light of Christ we look at the world—its exploding knowledge, peoples, revolutions, physical needs, desperate spiritual hunger and nakedness, and enslavement to false gods and demonic ideologies—we realize that Christian mission must certainly engage in many labors.

At various points he lists the excellent activities in which we must be engaged to fight war, injustice, poverty, ignorance, and exploitation. "A number of excellent enterprises lie around us. So great is the number and so urgent the calls, that Christians can easily lose their way among them, seeing them all equally as mission. But in doing the good, they can fail the best." He notes that "our Lord did not rest content with feeding the hungry and healing the sick. He pressed on to give His life a ransom for many and to send out His followers to disciple all nations."[12]

I got caught up in social issues. During the Vietnam war and civil rights struggle, Church Growth literature served to pull me back. More accurately, the correction was not "from" social concern but "to" social concern set more firmly in the context of the total Christian faith.

We must affirm the warning of Howard Snyder in his *The Community of the King,* "The numerical growth of a denomination does not further the Kingdom of God unless that denomination is faithful to the gospel in its internal community life, its worship and its witness in the world."[13]

Peter Wagner in his *Church Growth and the Whole Gospel: a Biblical Mandate* traced his own pilgrimage and that of many evangelicals. He quoted J. G. Davies who warned that "to define the goal of mission as church growth is to indulge in an ecclesiastical narrowing of the concept of the kingdom of God."[14] Wagner added, "Certainly no church growth advocate that I know would want to be guilty of narrowing either the concept of the kingdom of God or the command for its extension."[15]

The Matter of Terms

Part of the problem for some may be simply McGavran's use of the term "Church Growth."

He shied away from the term "evangelism" because he found it had come to mean everything good about the Christian faith. My own denomination allocated funds for work among Navajo alcoholics under the banner "evangelism." It was a good work, an important work, Christian work. Maybe it was evangelism. Maybe not.

In the sixties I attended a weeklong conference on evangelism at Green Lake, Wisconsin. Top denominational leaders were there. But it was all on the racial crisis and the scourge of war. These were important valid topics. But we were not dealing with evangelism in the fullest New Testament sense. We touched on *part* of the evangel, to be sure. But we were missing the heart of that term as used in the Scriptures. The conference took us down important roads, but it did not go far enough—not all the way to the foot of the cross. Christ must be Lord and Savior or our best efforts at peace and justice will shade off into blind alleys.

McGavran used the term "Church Growth."[16] "Growth" because that is what we are talking about—the extension of God's reign of love. And "Church" because it is not simply warm hearts, but people folded into a living, moving organism apart from which they quickly fade away.

I came to Church Growth as a skeptic. But I was intrigued because I had been looking for something like this since early in my ministry.

Discovering Stewardship Principles

The first congregation I served was in inner-city Harrisburg, Pennsylvania. At a time when many churches were relocating to the suburbs, it decided to stay in that spot. It decided to greatly expand its facilities and develop a seven-day-a-week program for those who lived in the shadows.

Skeptics said the young couples who lived in the suburbs would not support it. But the new, younger couples were excited about it while virtually every suburban person with accumulated wealth refused to have any part in it.

We had plans for a three-story air-conditioned Christian educational building with terazzo floors on the ground floor for neighborhood activities, a fellowship hall on top with a stage for drama, and an institutionally equipped kitchen. But we had no building fund. We knew that it all would have to come out of income.

We invited in Wayne Carr, a stewardship expert and a former pastor with skills at raising money. He spent several days in our congregation, looked at giving records, estimated incomes, and visited a number of key people. At the end of that time he said, "We can raise $100,000 over and above your regular giving over a three-year period, give or take a few percent either way, depending on uncertain variables."

We thought we were giving all we could. Some argued that a dedicated people automatically give and we did not need to pay someone to help us work at giving.

But our backs were against the wall. God had allowed a dream to capture us. We knew we could not do it on our own. We swallowed whatever hesitations we had and went with it.

At the end of three years we had received $104,000 over and above our regular giving. At the end of those three years we asked the stewardship expert to come back. He helped us to combine our building and regular fund and increase the giving level again.

Wayne Carr was able to do it because there are some principles of stewardship about which he knew. There is a theology behind it—assumptions about the individual and God. "We *need* to give," he said. "As frail human beings we need to give to God to express our dependence and our love far more than God needs to receive any gift we have to offer." There are also proven principles which can mean the difference between growth in stewardship and failure.

Carr taught us that we give out of a flow of income. He witnessed personally and directly about his own stewardship growth and about how it changed his life.

He talked very frankly. Because we were paying him a sizable fee, we listened to what he said and did what he asked. Because he was only there for an intense two weeks, he could talk directly to persons about "pocketbook protection" and confront their evasiveness without hesitation. If they got mad at him, he would soon be gone.

It was a rich experience, a time of genuine revival in every sense in that congregation, and one of the most meaningful pastoral experiences I have had.

But way back there I began to wonder, if there are *stewardship* princples, if there are things a trained person knows to do and not to do in that area, surely in the field of evangelism there must be some similar principles.

With my introduction to Win Arn, and through him to the Church Growth Movement, I found a systematic approach to what I had long felt must be possible. It was the fulfillment of a long-standing dream for me.

Testing

I have a friend who is a careful student of baseball. His brother, a coach, says that if you take a picture of the truly great hitters the moment the ball crosses the plate, you discover something interesting. No matter what their stance, no matter how they hold the bat or line up— whether batting out of a crouch like Pete Rose or circling the bat high overhead menacingly like a Dave Parker—at the moment of the swing, photos of the great ones indicate that the position of their hands, the bat level, and the weight distribution are all the same. They all came to the plate with their own style, but at the "moment of truth," the great ones had mastered some key responses which checked out to be very much the same.

Pastors come in all styles: tall, short, loud, soft-spoken. Churches use different "languages" to describe the faith they hold. But those that grow, we are discovering, have some things in common.

Jack Dempsey was taken to see a newcomer to the box-ing profession who seemed to have all the makings of a champion. He was big. He was fast. He was muscular. He worked out daily. He kept in training. He showed good form at the punching bag. "This boy sure can box," he was told. Dempsey's response was, "It's not so much what you can do, but that you can do it on Saturday night at ten o'clock in Madison Square Garden."

The moods of a Church Growth person are 1) obedi-ence, 2) pragmatism, and 3) optimism. They know they are called to be faithful. They are optimistic about the future God can give. And they are open and flexible, ready to dis-card methods which do not accomplish what they are at-tempting to do. The goals do not change. But the tools to share the faith may grow dull or irrelevant. And if so, they must be sharpened or replaced by other, better tools.

Three Streams

Peter Wagner in his classes traces three streams of evangelism. In the 1950s we saw an emphasis on "crusade evangelism." It began in 1949 with a telegram from news-paper owner William Randolph Hearst after young Billy Graham preached in the Los Angeles area. Two words helped launch that young evangelist on his way. "Puff Graham," telegrammed Hearst to his newspaper chain. And they did.

And what an exciting era it was. Win Arn who himself

had worked for Youth for Christ reflects upon that period in the film *Reach Out and Grow*. He also looks back with some concerns about it.

Studies began to be made to see how many people who came forward in those meetings ever found their way into the life of the church and were nurtured from babies to full-grown Christians. The best studies showed that far too few ever made the transition.

In the 1960s there was a change in methods. Ken Strachan, the son of a great Latin-American evangelist, wanted to reduce the high infant mortality rate among newborn Christians. He developed "Evangelism in Depth," which later came to be known as "saturation evangelism."[17] Peter Wagner was a young missionary in Bolivia at the time. He thrilled to the efforts to train and send evangelists to communities. At that time there were something like 60,000 believers in Bolivia. As a result of the effort, 20,000 new decisions were made.

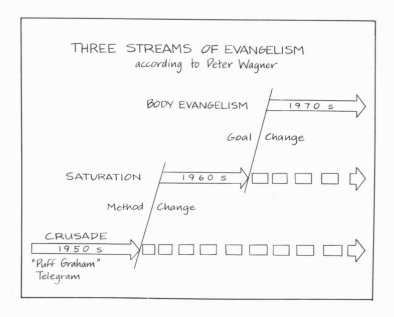

As Wagner prepared for his furlough and deputation work in the States he had made many notes and taken many pictures. He had what he thought were probably the most impressive missionary lectures ever produced. Back at Fuller Theological Seminary at the outset of his furlough, he happened to talk to one of the Church Growth professors, Ralph Winter, who casually asked if Wagner had seen the studies made on saturation evangelism and the longer-term results. Wagner said he had not. Winter suggested it might be worth looking at. Wagner pulled out the studies and to his dismay saw that the final result was not that good. In some instances, denominations which had been growing transferred their energies to saturation evangelism. The long-term result was a plateauing, rather than increased or even continuing growth.

Things began to shift again. This time the shift was not in terms of method but in terms of goal, a shift to what some called "body evangelism." Some began to realize that the church is the nursery where new Christians must be received and learn to walk and talk and take their first bites of solid food. Evangelism which produces lasting results must be through the body, not separated from it.

Church Growth people sometimes talk of "three-P evangelism."

A lot of good people practice what is called "presence evangelism." Presence evangelism is being there, being good people, living good lives. The assumption is that people will see our witness and because of our own loving, caring lifestyle will want to become Christian, too.

One of the problems with that is that none of us is that good. Not even Jesus Christ was willing to simply let his good life be the only witness. We point to one far beyond us, not to our own goodness. Else we are both deceived and mistakenly proud.

Another problem is that talking is a part of living. If we share our lives but not with our lips, we are withholding what is a natural part of all human experience.

PRESENCE
EVANGELISM

PROCLAMATION
EVANGELISM

PERSUASION
EVANGELISM

A second approach is "proclamation evangelism." Billy Graham represents this approach. "Here's life"[18] was an example. *Decisions* are sought. One problem with this is that the New Testament does not talk of seeking decisions. But 263 times (count 'em) it talks about making disciples.

A third approach might be called "persuasion evangelism." This involves going beyond decisions to *making disciples*. It assumes that evangelism is not complete until converts are "responsible members of Christ's church." This approach is based on research, not on wishful thinking. It does not use "canned" methods borrowed from someone else. Rather, it encourages each congregation to discover its own strengths and to develop strategies growing out of its own situation and resources.

Actually, good evangelism involves all three P's. There must be a *presence*. People must know us and trust us and want to discover what has found meaning for us. Presence *is* a part of all evangelism.

And *proclamation* is a part. We must talk about it. But we must go on to the final part, *persuasion*, folding people into the life of the church. We must use our best understandings to develop our strategies and evangelistic methods.

The exciting new world of Church Growth actually is less a closed package of ideology into which one must buy than it is a mood, an openness, an approach. It combines the nature of our faith together with the realization that God gave us minds and creative skills and expects us to use them fully in his service.

As a Lutheran pastor friend in Indiana, newly into Church Growth materials, said to me, "I just decided I shouldn't have to invent the wheel myself." Why not draw on the trials and errors, the best thinking, and the accumulated wisdom of other intelligent, concerned Christians?

On a Scale of One to Ten

Does this mean that I am ready to swallow the findings and theory of Donald McGavran whole, case closed, truth in a bundle all tied up with no questions asked?

Not at all. As I became more deeply involved in the studies and findings, I discovered that there is wide-rang-ing discussion at many points. Students of McGavran, like Peter Wagner, sometimes say, "I question McGavran at this point." Or, "I don't agree on that." Of course, Wagner will also criticize Wagner.

One time I listened to a spirited debate at Fuller Theological Seminary on the question, "Is the Church Growth movement biblically sound?" A colleague from the theology department quoted an earlier book by Wagner. With some delight the professor questioned some of Peter's statements. He read several choice paragraphs and "took them apart." When Peter Wagner responded, he simply said, "I wrote that several years ago, and I have changed my thinking on that. I don't agree with it either."

YESTERDAY I WAS SO SURE

There is in the movement as a whole an openness, a willingness to question, and an eagerness to receive thoughtful criticism which I have not found very many other places.

If a harsh criticism appears in some publication, Peter

Wagner will tell his students, "This is an article you need to read." As a student, I used to feel the need to defend the movement. But their attitude is, "No, we want to be corrected, to hear all valid criticisms."

But the test of the Church Growth ideas has come in even harsher ways for me. I serve two small churches in southern California. One lost 58 percent of its membership during the period from 1965 to 1977. The other lost 85 percent of its membership.

As I worked these fields for a year or two, I soon discovered that my best efforts were producing little. For them the discouragement was too real, the hurts too deep, the bad memories too deeply ingrained.

I went to my first Church Growth seminar knowing I needed better answers than I had. I went with the same seriousness that a young couple goes to a counselor when their marriage is breaking up and they desperately want it saved.

Part of the problem was momentum. Things were on dead center. One pastor of a growing small church said, "It has gotten easy. People live with expectancy. They're willing to try new things, always reaching out."

I recall the story of Robert Fulton and his newly created steamship, the *Claremont*. A group of people gathered on the river to watch him demonstrate that it really would run. One old farmer in the group, a veteran of life and its realities, shook his head and commented, "He'll never get 'er started." But he did "get 'er started." The steam began to pour out and the boat actually began to move. Slowly at first. Then faster. Faster and faster it went. The old farmer turned to the person beside him, shook his head sadly and said, "He'll never get 'er stopped."

We're talking about *inertia* here. The truth that things at rest tend to remain at rest has been engraved on my being from the early years in my current pastorates. After I went there, I learned that the people had all agreed to "try it for just one more year." They were ready to close up, but they were willing—skeptically—to see if this fella could do anything about it.

But my best efforts were not enough. So as I came to Church Growth, I came like a hungry man looking for food or a thirsty man in search of water. And I came testing. The theories and very formulations were for me not just so many mind-titilating ideas on a page. I did not care if it sounded good or had a good ring to it or if it seemed plausible. I needed to know, would it work? Was it abstract theory or was it as basic as mashed potatoes? Was it as solid as the earth itself?

So across the past months and years I have taken each idea, each suggestion, each concept, and carefully measured it against my own best understanding of the gospel. I have tested it in the hard crucible of life. Some of the things may work well elsewhere. Some may have immeasurable value in West Africa or Hong Kong or Bolivia. But for me in my setting with the people among whom I labor today and tomorrow, not all have been helpful. Other ideas are immediately valid.

So what I write about is not theory only. It is as real as life.

If you were to cross the threshold into the churches I serve, you would see that we have a long way to go. Part of it is because we have a lot of hurt from which to recover. Part of it is because God did not give those churches a perfect pastor or perfect people. A large part of it is that we are not always able to *do* the good that we *know*. We know some of the things that make for growth. *Some* of them we do. Some of them we have not been able to convince ourselves to do.

It is like many people who struggle with weight that is five, ten, fifteen, or more pounds above what it ought to be. Or my lawn which needs feeding and reseeding in spots. Other priorities crowd out getting done what I know I should.

We are imperfect people in an imperfect world with

many conflicting pulls. But some things are basic, proven, and true. They simply await being tested, tried, and done.

So, are we getting ourselves too heavily involved in work that belongs to God alone? *Are* we, in fact, trying to program the Holy Spirit?

In a garden, we all know that God gives the growth. No one could imagine for a minute that any human can produce a seed which will bring forth the vegetables we enjoy. We can't even create a radish. But God does it not without our effort. Soil preparation, fertilizer, seed, water, choosing the right location—all are a part of our responsibility.

I heard of a man who visited a beautiful landscaped garden and commented, "Just look what God could have done if only he had had more money."

That's not it. In the providence of God, some tasks on earth have been assigned to us. The raw materials are here. But some of the doing awaits our hands.

The apostle Paul was well aware that God gives the increase in his church, but not without human effort. "I planted the seed, Apollos watered," Paul noted. But ultimately the growth comes from God (1 Corinthians 3:6, TEV).

In the same way, no medical doctor heals. Doctors do not heal us. A doctor may set a broken bone or stitch torn skin or remove an obstruction or growth. But the doctor does not heal. God gives the healing. His healing forces are always at work within us. A doctor simply creates the conditions (hopefully) where healing can take place.

So we work together. God has called us into his kingdom to share with him in his grand design of helping his children live together in love for him and at peace with themselves and each other.

As for me, I know I need all the insight, all the understanding, and suggestions I can get. God wants from me my very best for his all-important tasks.

Why Did All the Growing Stop?

Why is it that all of the mainline churches which had grown all across their history suddenly quit growing?

In one twelve-year period—between 1965 and 1977—the congregations of my own denomination, the Church of the Brethren, in Southern California, lost together 41 percent of their membership. They were in the best of company!

At about the same time the United Methodist Church nationally was losing one million, two hundred thousand members. The Disciples of Christ were losing about one-third of their membership across the country.

Membership graphs of the United Church of Christ and the Presbyterians the Lutheran Church in America and the American Lutheran Church and the others mentioned above show differing heights for the peak of the late sixties. But the pattern is much the same. There was slow steady growth in the early years and more rapid growth just before the beginning of this century. A peak in the mid-sixties was then followed by a decline.[1]

"It's just the times," some will say. "Churchgoing was popular in the Eisenhower years. People aren't interested in church today." "Things have changed. Homes are breaking up. People are having less children. The mood is different." We could (and do) say all those things. And there is some truth in each statement.

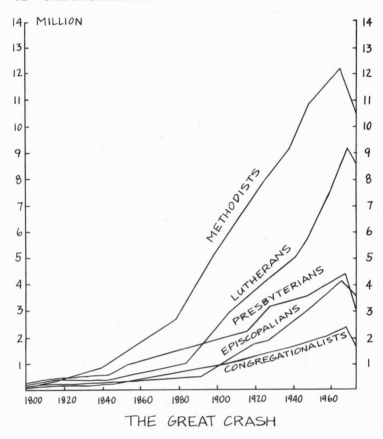

In fact, there is a helpful book by Hoge (pronounced like you would a submarine sandwich—ho'-gee) and Roozen, *Understanding Church Growth and Decline: 1950-1979.*[2] It is a thick book and ponderous in parts. The suggestion in its pages is that four factors converged like pieces of a puzzle to cause the sudden dropping off.[3]

There has been convulsive change around us. Hoge and Roozen talk of contextual factors: the cultural context in which we must labor. They talk about *national contextual* factors—things like the Vietnam War, racial turmoil, the homosexual revolution, changes in home and family life, and women's struggles which swept the entire nation. They talk also of the impact of *local contextual* factors— the mood and changes in our own communities over which we many times had little or no control.

They add to these two institutional factors. *National institutional* factors—the directions of top denominational leadership—had a major bearing on what happened. And *local institutional* factors—the direction of local leaders: pastor, board, members—played an important role. These four elements fit together to produce much of whatever change there was.

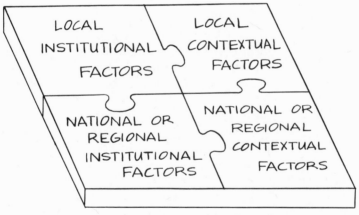

FACTORS AFFECTING CHURCH GROWTH

It would be easy to wash our hands sadly and say that decline is inevitable in these trying, uncertain times. However, while some congregations and some entire denominations were losing members hand over fist, other congregations (even in declining denominations) and other whole denominations were growing.

It took the Mormons 100 years to get their first million members. It took them 20 years to get their second million members, 10 years to win their third million, and four years their fourth million. They are now growing at the rate of about a million members a year. The growth is there: solid, big, impressive. In the face of impressive decline by others.

Pastor Cal Keeling served a Church of the Brethren in Bakersfield, California. Across the street at the opposite end of the block was a Mormon church. On Sunday mornings their parking was spilling over onto his lot.

(I heard of a Baptist church in Michigan which had this problem with some Methodists nearby and worked at the problem by having bumper stickers printed which they put on the bumper of every "visiting" Methodist car: "I'm *proud* to be a Baptist!")

Cal Keeling worked at it more directly. He paid them a visit, said they were glad to have them as neighbors, but that they must stop using their parking lot. Their response was, "Why? It's just a matter of time and it will all be ours anyway."

Why did all the growing stop for some but not for others?

I have a Lutheran pastor friend in the Midwest who comments that the charts of their losses are presented at their synod meetings as "good news." Compared to the Methodists, they have lost so many fewer members.

A second grade public school teacher was having her students watch the process of baby chicks trying to break out of their shells under the warm light of an incubator. The teacher said to them, "Isn't it amazing how they chip their way out of those shells?"

One little boy responded, "What wonders me is how they got in there in the first place."

How did we get ourselves in the fix we are in? Can the process be reversed? How do we get things turned around again?

Church Growth theoretician Peter Wagner (who contributed a chapter to the book by Hoge and Roozen) suggests that many factors played a part, but that *one key shift* may have been pivotal. In the sixties, in the face of turmoil abroad and at home, the Vietnam War, racial struggles, and all the rest, top denominational leaders in many so-called mainline churches shifted the first priority from "making disciples" to correcting social injustice. The emphasis became different and the program became different. For one thing new congregations were no longer being planted. While the Southern Baptists were starting new churches at the rate of one a day for ten years, many other church bodies almost completely ceased such activity, despite the fact that the population was continuing to grow and new communities were opening up all over the place. Indeed, some mainline denominational executives suggest that this shift *alone*—the simple failure to continue planting new churches—would have been enough to shut off growth.

New opportunities were lost. But studies also indicate that churches, like people, tend to grow rapidly when they are young and fresh. As they mature, they level off and stop reaching out. They feel that they have given their time and their energies. They are ready to sit back, rest, and enjoy. The growing edge of denominations for the most part are the newer congregations.

Many church groups have shifted energies and emphasis. We experienced a terrible war, heart-rending examples of injustice in our own land, and poverty in our own backyards. The social unrest bubbling up all around us began more and more to consume our first attention. It was right that we were concerned. But in the process we almost forgot the mandate not only to *be* disciples but to also *make* disciples. More and more we took our cue from the cover stories of *Newsweek* and *Time*.

"Let the world write the agenda,"[4] was the stirring cry. Jesus was proclaimed, after a phrase from Bonhoeffer, "the man for others."[5] A hurting humanity consumed us.

Personal decisions, worship, and building up the body of Christ would have to wait.

I heard D. T. Niles of India speak in that period to a gathering of the General Board of the National Council of Churches. He said that Jesus was not primarily a "man for others." He was, first of all, "a man for his Father." For Jesus, the *world* did not write the agenda. *God* wrote the agenda. Niles' point was that the difference, although it might seem slight, in the longer haul can be tremendous.

If Wagner is right, if the critical cause for a decline in membership is a shift from disciple making to a priority on social issues, what is the answer?

Shall we shut our eyes to injustice and refuse to address the problems of hunger and war and abuse? Not at all, suggests Wagner. *"Keep social concern high.* Do not minimize it. But let disciple-making become the *first* priority once again." If you do, he argues, not only will you begin to grow in members again, but you will find that social concern is even stronger. And he has set out to collect evidence that this educated hunch is right.

One of the problems is that the shift was subtle at first, but is now deeply established. Many church leaders are less than convinced about the value and role of the institutional church.

One church leader, meeting with a committee studying the loss in his small denomination, said, "I'm not sure that a (190,000 member) church with 50,000 less members than it has today might not be more faithful, stronger, more desirable." He was assuming that the loss would be of the unfaithful and that those who remained would be the dynamic, committed, and truly faithful.

Some church and religious executives and even some pastors have become *"translocal."* They jet-hop across the country and around the world. They find fellowship among other professionals. They no longer draw their life and inspiration from the local congregation. Indeed, they find congregations a waste of time, a necessary burden.

Some are not convinced that life is to be found in Jesus Christ. There is a new openness to truth from any source. Persons must be free to find their own way. Pluralism is

NOW I'M SAFE !

embraced uncritically. A kind of religious agnosticism has replaced deep personal conviction.

One indication of this is that many who have held top posts in the religious world virtually leave the church when they retire. It was a professional thing with them, not a burning passion. When their professional career came to an end, they began to putter at other things, virtually indifferent to the "movement and magnificence" into which they were called.

Can churches turn it around? Can holes be plugged, ships refitted, and the voyage reinitiated?

Dean Kelley in a most important book, *Why Conservative Churches Are Growing,* says it is not likely. Kelley says his book is misnamed. He wanted something like, "Why churches that *make demands* are growing." His thesis, quite simply, is that churches that make demands are strong and that strong churches grow.[6]

His book recalled a statement in the New Testament. Following the Sermon on the Mount and again early in Mark and Luke, the Gospel writers say, "The crowds were astonished at his teaching, for he taught them as one who had authority" (Matthew 7:29, RSV; see also Mark 1:22; Luke 4:32).

In college and seminary, some of my professors would say, "Some people say this ... and other people say that...." When you asked what *they* say, they would refuse to commit themselves. This kind of attitude is easily carried over into preaching. On hot issues, not wanting to step into a buzz saw, it is much easier to share views of sticky theological issues than to commit oneself.

I had a delightful, bright young couple who came all the way from the Foursquare Gospel Church to the Church of the Brethren, questioning and testing all the way. Dick used to get upset when on something very important to him I seemed to hedge. Once he referred to me as "wishy-washy Wayne Zunkel." That playful little phrase stung and stayed with my memory.

I know a wonderful pastor who was loved by his people. But one of his parishioners once said to me, "He preaches a tremendous sermon the first fifteen minutes. But if the topic is somewhat controversial, he takes it all away in the last five minutes. He wants to be on both sides of every important issue."

Hungry people want bread. Hurting, lost, struggling people want to know. When I go to the doctor, I want to know what is wrong.

Kelley discovered that some of the denominational leaders in declining churches thought that their social concern was the cause of their loss.

Rev. Robert Schuller, speaking to the United Methodist Congress on Evangelism, contended that churches were empty because ministers insisted on "talking about social ethics in Sunday services" ... instead of addressing "psychological hurts and needs." The place for ethical discussions is "in the classroom," Schuller said.[7]

But Dean Kelley has the figures of actual studies to show that the people themselves were not opposed to churches declaring themselves on social or personal sins, *if* it was done in the context of the larger faith. People are hungry, first of all, for *ultimate meaning.* They want to understand the nature of life and death, who they are, how they fit into God's plan. Lay people by and large do not object to a church or a pastor who speaks out strongly "out of faith, with a firm faith undergirding" about the issues of our times.[8]

In more formal language, Karl Barth says, "There is no wisdom in stopping at the next-to-the-last and the next-to-the-next-to-the-last want of people; and they will not thank us for doing so." Our people have high expectations. "They expect us to understand them better than they understand themselves, and to take them more seriously than they take themselves."[9]

Pastors and church leaders want to be kind. But it was the great English pastor Studdert-Kennedy who suggested that in trying to be kinder than Christ, we can cease to be kind at all.[10]

Says Barth, "We are unfeeling, not when we probe deeply into the wound they carry when they come to us for healing, but rather when we pass over it as if we did not know why they had come."

"Single, bold strokes are OK, but they shouldn't be rushed into!"

People want it straight. "We are misled not when we assume that they are brought to us by the last and profoundest questions, but rather when we think that when they come to us they may really be put off with next-to-the-last and less profound answers."

People are hungry. And "if we do not understand this ultimate desire," says Barth, "if we do *not* take the people seriously (I repeat it, more seriously than they take themselves!) at the point of their life perplexity, we need not wonder if a majority of them, without becoming enemies of the church, gradually learn to leave the church to itself and us to the kind-hearted and timid."

Barth becomes downright nasty: "Is it psychologically strange that the more wide-awake sons of ministers and theologians continue to join this silent army of deserters?" He suggests a most unkind reason: "Do they not do so because they know from close observation that people will hardly find in our churches what they are really seeking? Am I not at least partly right when I say that people, educated and uneducated alike, are simply disappointed in us, unspeakably disappointed?"[11]

Examples of strength

The examples which Kelley uses of strong churches that grew are, first of all, those of the Anabaptist movement and second, the Wesley movement.[12] Neither was narrowly personal nor pietistic. Both were concerned about the injustice of their times. The Anabaptists had a strong witness against war from the outset. The Wesleys were concerned with the poor and the dispossessed. For both, it was a full gospel—personal and social.

The key is addressing the *major questions*, not neglecting the deep hungers of the heart for ultimate meaning. Many pastors can say from experience, you can talk about almost anything and take a strong position if it comes out of a firm biblical base. But if it is only your own idea, forget it.

One major factor is the church's own sense of conviction, its "seriousness/strictness/costliness/bindingness," to use Kelley's words.[13]

Kelley goes on to say that there is a hunger for faith-grounded, socially conscious Christians. The "conservative" pool has been about used up.[14] There are many, many people who want the church to address the issues of our time, but who are presently outside the church.

In southern California there are rich mega-congregations who have no social concern for the hurting people around them—no clothing banks or food banks for those whose homes burn down or who are suddenly in need of temporary help.

If some of the mainline congregations and denominations could get their act together and get cured of the fever of trying to be all things to all people (and therefore ending up being very little to anybody), they would find they have a market out there for what they might have to offer.

Can churches which have shifted priorities and lost a vision regain it? The Scriptures talk about sounding an uncertain trumpet and getting no response (1 Corinthians 14:8). Can people who have a shaky lip ever again blow the trumpet with certainty?

It is *possible*, certainly. Losers have regrouped and regained a vision and begun to march again. But Kelley says that while it is possible, it is unlikely. He uses the word "dying" to describe what is happening to many of us. He uses the word by deliberate choice because, he says, "the process we see at work in the churches is probably not reversible. Having once succumbed to debility," having allowed themselves to grow weak, "a church is unlikely to recover, but not because measures leading to recovery could not be prescribed and instituted." (Later in his book Kelley lists some steps that could be taken, and other onlookers can make specific prescriptions.) But the *probability* is that they will continue to die "because the persons who now occupy positions of leadership and followership in the church will not find them congenial and will not want to institute them. They prefer a church which is not too strenuous or demanding—a church, in fact, which is dying."[15]

I once served on a committee studying the declining membership of my own denomination, the Church of the Brethren. Our committee suggested specific steps to be taken at every level—national, judicatory, local, and personal. I am convinced that if even a handful of the things suggested were taken seriously, the direction of the church could change dramatically. It has been most interesting to me to see what will happen. It's like a doctor holding a cure to a person's physical infirmity. He says, "It will involve some pain, some discomfort. It will not heal you immediately. It will involve a vigorous program of physical therapy and a strict diet for a period of time. It will involve sacrifice and great determination on your part. But it is possible. The choice is in your hands."

Would we do it if the choice were personal life or death? Would we do it if the choice were life or death for the congregation that we know and love? Would we do it for convictions which are unique to our own faith and tradition, which we feel are basic to the Christian gospel?

I believe that some are genuinely convinced that turn-around is not possible. The exterior forces are too great, the mood too unfriendly, the cultural conditions too alien.

In 1986, the Methodists' biennial Congress on Evangelism noted that membership for that body had dropped for the 21st straight year. Sunday school attendance was one-half of what it was two decades before. Two-thirds of the 38,000 churches did not have confirmation or membership classes. In 1984, one-third of the congregations failed to baptize a single new member.

"We're tired, listless, full of nostalgia for earlier days," said Arkansas Bishop Richard B. Wilke, who chaired a special membership growth committee in a speech to the congress.[15]

I was most intrigued by Alan K. Waltz's book *Images of the Future*, which describes the results of the United Methodist church's Delphi panel, named after the ancient oracle.[16] I'm especially intrigued because it seems to run counter to the heroic efforts of their former top evangelism staff person, George Hunter III, who was convinced that their great denomination could reverse fields and grow again.

The picture I get from their panel of 133 experts is that the great denomination knows what to do, but like at tormented giant, it doubts that it is willing to do it.

Waltz says in his book that the panel sees "a denomination primarily concerned with administering its past and describing the symptoms of its present malaise, but unwilling to seek a better understanding of its discomfort or to take the requisite steps to effect a cure." Waltz notes that "this pessimistic outlook will prevail only if events are allowed to run their course without intervention." He presents issues which, by the way they are dealt with, "will determine the future effectiveness, if not the survival, of The United Methodist Church."[18]

The panel predicts increased diversity of beliefs among the denomination and seems to assume that the church's taking a clear stand on moral and theological issues, even if based on the spiritual and moral values of the Christian faith, would mean a loss of membership.[19]

The assumption among so many is that to grow, a church must go with the flow of culture. Hoge and Roozen say the opposite. They insist that those churches which are growing are those with strong convictions. *Acute acculturation* seems to characterize the churches that are *not* growing. "The membership losses have been greatest," say Hoge and Roozen, "in those denominations 1) filled with cosmopolitan middle-class persons and 2) maintaining minimal distance if any, from the life-style and morality of mainstream American culture."[20]

Olden Mitchell, an Indiana pastor, chaired his denomination's study committee in this area. Based on vast reading and study, he makes the following six observations in an unpublished paper, "Some Perspectives on Church Growth and Decline in America:"

1. The declining denominations tend to be "typically culture-affirming and supportive of the social status quo."[21] In other words, watering down one's faith has not attracted people. Rather, it turns them off and turns them away.

2. In dying denominations, there is great confusion and uncertainty as to the faith, the meaning of faith, and the meaning of Christian discipleship. "If the mainline churches could muster sufficient seriousness about what they profess to believe, they might cease to be blown from pillar to post by every breeze of cultural climate," writes Dean Kelley. "They might even begin to affect some of the circumstances around them, to influence the cultural climate themselves, as their forefathers did." These churches, said Kelley, need "to ask themselves what, if anything, they are prepared to be serious about, and then do it."[22]

3. Hoge and Roozen argue that the "national changes in church participation in the past two decades" is, contrary to popular belief, not due primarily to *demographic* changes—such a migration, urbanization, educational trends—but to *religious* climate."[23]

4. It is not from without but from *within* that the problem must first be seen. To the eyes of the multitudes, "there is an inescapable and overwhelming impression that the church is ... lacking in warmth, personal concern, openness, and acceptance." The masses of unchurched people are saying "that the institutional church is not effective in helping people find meaning in life; is not warm or accepting of outsiders; ... is too concerned about organizational issues; has lost the real spiritual part of religion."[24]

5. Olden Mitchell said that we do what we *plan* to do, as

persons, as congregations, and as denominations. We move in the direction of achieving what we set out to do. The denomination which is declining in membership *has not had a master plan or strategy* through which it focuses its energies in a determined effort to grow. It has not given evangelism, sharing the faith, and making disciples a very high priority in the past two or more decades. In the churches that are declining, the "membership trends are more the result of failure of recruitment of new members than of the dropping out of existing members."[25] Said Mitchell, "Churches that don't plan to grow don't grow. They decline!"

6. Among many in the declining denominations there is a kind of helplessness or indifference toward sin. Early in my ministry I attended a weekly workshop, one day a week, across some eight weeks on the problem of alcoholism. It was conducted in a city hospital drawing together people from the medical profession, psychologists, clergy, and state government resource people. One of the things they told us which I accepted without question across all my ministry was that an alcoholic must reach "psychological bottom" before help will be sought or accepted. You cannot really help them, we were told, until they recognize their need and genuinely want help and ask for help.

Later, I read an article on a new approach to alcoholism: *"Intervention, a new first step to help."*[26] It told of a man being called into his boss's office to find his two grown sons, his boss, and a man dressed in clergy clothes (someone he had never met before).

He immediately thought to himself, "Nothing could be wrong with my wife because I just left her 30 minutes ago." He was right. Nothing had happened to his wife. The group that greeted him had gathered to tell him what had happened *to him*—that he was an alcoholic and in desperate need of help. The approach is based on a relatively new theory that family members and others close to an alcoholic can *intervene,* can bring pressure to lead a person to recognize the problem and seek help for it.

It was the opposite of what I had been taught and had faithfully believed and acted upon across some 20 years of ministry.

And it applies not only to alcohol! I can remember my dad as a pastor going down to the local bar to talk to a member with gambling fever in his veins. The man had received a paycheck and immediately headed down to gamble it away. Meanwhile, the children played around the house without shoes and his wife could not scrape together enough money for food. My dad walked right in, sat down by Ed, looked him squarely in the eye, and said, "Ed, you don't want to be here. You are destroying the things you love the most. You want to come out now and go home with me to your wife and children who love you."

And Ed went. But we have gotten away from that kind of confrontation. "Too judgmental," we thought. We were "assuming authority" which we felt we did not have. "We didn't want to get too involved where we had no business."

Whether the problem was adultery or dishonesty or simply staying away from church, we have felt that each person is doing, as one of our church leaders told me when I was growing up, "about as good as he or she can." Each person must come to rock bottom first. When they are ready, they will ask for help. Only then can we help them.

Counseling, of course, was all Rogerian. Pastors simply reflected whatever any one said. It was never directive.

And yet in my home I never believed this. I believed that every child should listen to parents not because the parents are so wise. Certainly not because parents are so good. But simply because parents have been around for awhile.

Somewhere between the past's judgmental, pushy attitude and today's indifference, there must be a better way. "Intervention"—thought out, solid, careful, honest—must hold some keys for us as we approach a world which is too big and pressures which are too strong.

Olden Mitchell says, "There is a gross indifference among many in the declining denominations toward those who are burdened with sin, and seeming unawareness of the lostness experienced by multitudes of people today."[27] Or it may be a lack of concern for people, an indifference to the spiritual hungers of persons. As the spiritually starving seek food, they frequently bypass many churches—or these churches bypass them.

"How can we grow in such an alien culture?" a concerned, faithful pastor asked me recently. "The world does not believe what we believe. Its values are so different. If we are faithful to our Lord and the New Testament, won't we of necessity be small?"

My mind immediately went back to the New Testament church. It had no resources. It was terribly small. At first there was only a handful. They had no sympathy from outsiders—not in the community nor among other religious groups nor among those in government.

Ridiculed, attacked, and abused, they did not try to bend their convictions to the pagan world around them so that they might succeed. They preached Jesus wherever they went. They did not go where the climate was good. "In season and out of season," they shared the radiant good news which burned in their hearts and brought joy to their faces (2 Timothy 4:2). And despite it all, they grew. Maybe in part *because* of it all they grew.

The door is open. The necessary steps are known. What is needed is a vision, the willingness, the will.

A key word must surely be *determination.* How much do we want to grow?

Jamaal Wilkes, a professional basketball player whose grace earned him the nickname "Silk" and whose talent made him an important part of four NBA championship teams, retired early. During his most productive years, Jamaal had played for the world champion Los Angeles Lakers. Later he played for the struggling Los Angeles Clippers.

When asked why he was quitting, Wilkes gave several reasons. But the key may have been when he said of playing with the Clippers, "The job here is to play. With the Lakers, the job is to win. It's a big difference. It's a mental thing, an attitude. With the Lakers, every practice is a happening, an event. They know they're going to win. Here, it's just the reverse. The Clippers have solid personnel, but they're a lousy team as far as their record is concerned."[28]

Little growth will come until we determine that we really do intend to grow.

Chapter 7 ·

That Offensive Homogeneous Principle

One of the key discoveries of Donald McGavran about why and how churches grow is the "homogeneous principle."[1] Among many church people it has had a terrible press.

Simply stated, McGavran's observation is that "people like to become Christians without crossing significant linguistic, ethnic, or cultural barriers."[2] People like to hear the gospel in their own mother tongue. They respond more readily, McGavran was saying, if it is presented to them in containers with which they are familiar and with which they feel at home.

A Korean Church of the Brethren meets in the Panorama City church which I serve. It has its services in Korean. Many of its members speak no English. They sing our hymns, but the words are all in Korean. Almost weekly they include meals in their gatherings. The food is Korean.

Our congregation could put a sign out front, "Koreans are welcome," which they are. (As a matter of fact, our English-speaking Panorama church had one Korean family. The wife spoke almost no English. The boy, eleven, refused to speak Korean.) They are warmly welcomed in our services. But the hard truth is, unless the sign were in Korean, they wouldn't even know what it said.

McGavran early discovered and stated this rather simple observation. Cultures are different. And sometimes the cultural container has more to do with keeping people from accepting the gospel than anything in the gospel.[3]

But how he has stirred anger by that observation! Hell hath no fury like a Christian with shattered illusions.

In 1974, Ralph Winter of the faculty of the School of World Mission at Fuller Seminary presented a paper at the plenary session of the International Congress of Evangelism in Lausanne, Switzerland, on the homogeneous principle. The next day, a newspaper in race-conscious South Africa proclaimed, "Fuller Seminary Endorses Apartheid." Somehow recognizing people's right to their own peoplehood was interpreted as advocating separation of the races.

A Lutheran appraisal of the entire Church Growth movement focused primarily on the homogeneous principle. In *LCA Partners*, N. Amanda Grimmer acknowledged that "it is a fact that people gather in Homogeneous Units." But, she criticized, "It is more comfortable that way for sinful human beings who do not like to cross 'racial, linguistic, or class barriers' for any reason, including worship of the Triune God." She continued, "Although we redeemed but sinful human beings prefer to gather in Homogeneous Units, it is a mistake to confuse our preference with what the Spirit intends."[4]

A winsome, brilliant woman, who was the former executive of the Florida and Puerto Rico District of the Church of the Brethren, led a group of district executives in a discussion of the loss of membership in the denomination. She prefaced all she wanted to say about Church Growth with the assertion, "I want to make it clear that I completely reject the Homogeneous Principle." Yet as she continued to share at the midmorning break, she indicated that she intended to spend four weeks at a little town—Cuernavaca—in Mexico this summer (like she had done the previous summer), where, at some expense, she might master the Spanish language as her district reaches out with vigor to plant new congregations in

Puerto Rico and among Spanish-speaking peoples in Florida.

She was a living, enthusiastic, wonderful example of the truth she was rejecting so harshly with her lips.

The private confirmation of many who "reject it outright" is that "it is true," but "I frankly do not like it and reject it as a statement of Christian intention."

Ways Cultures Relate

In his classes Peter Wagner suggests seven ways in which dominant cultures relate to less dominant cultures.

First, *genocide.* Hitler tried it with the Jews. We saw an example in our own lifetime in Cambodia. In early America, this was the policy toward Indians. There were more than a few whites who felt that the only good Indian was a dead Indian.

Second, *deportation.* Idi Amin exercised this policy toward East Indians in Uganda. Many in the U.S. felt this way toward Iranians during the hostage crisis. There are those in our country who have advocated repatriation of blacks from our shores.

Third, *apartheid,* legal separation of the races. We see it attempted in South Africa. There are many towns in our own land which up into the 1960s had laws that no black might be on their streets after sundown.

Four, *structural racism.* Group contact is considered antisocial. Former President Carter's own church in Plains, Georgia, split over attitudes toward accepting blacks. There was no law, but there was tremendous social pressure.

Five, *assimilationist racism.* Other races are simply absorbed. The end result of assimilationist racism is genocide, the death of a culture, of a unique people. This is the most prevalent kind of racism today. It is what Japan tried to do to Korea for 36 years. The Korean language was prohibited. Names were changed into Japanese characters. Korean men were forced to marry Japanese women.

WAYS CULTURES RELATE

GENOCIDE

DEPORTATION

APARTHEID

Six, the best of all worlds: an *open society*. Wagner says he would like to think this is what America is becoming. A place where cultural integrity is safeguarded but where social mobility is entirely free.

Seven, *secession*. Voluntary independence. We see the

STRUCTURAL RACISM

ASSIMILATION

OPEN SOCIETY

SECESSION

BLACK IS
BEAUTIFUL!

struggle among Puerto Ricans and among those of French Quebec. In time there may be pressure for a Navajo nation. The momentum of six sometimes leads to seven.

Seeking Unity in a Multilingual Setting

René Padilla is a harsh critic of the homogeneous unit

principle. Padilla is right when he contends, "Throughout the entire New Testament the oneness of the people of God as a oneness that transcends all outward distinctions is taken for granted.[5] But Padilla misunderstands when he suggests, for example, that "a modern Church Growth expert might have" tried to solve the Hellenist question (Acts 6:1) by suggesting "the creation of two distinct denominations, one for Palestinian Jews and another for Greek Jews."[6]

When Padilla argues that "no suggestion is ever given (in the New Testament) that Jewish Christians preached the gospel to 'none except Jews' *because of strategic considerations,*" he misunderstands a setting where there are differing cultures and languages. By the very attempt to reach out to one language or culture you do *(without attempting to)* turn another aside, unless you intentionally attempt to also reach out to them.

Padilla quotes John Poulton on the goal of the church. "When masters could call slaves brothers, when the enormities of depersonalizing them became conscious in enough people's minds, something had to go. It took time, but slavery went. And in the interim, the people of God were an embodied question—more because here were people who could live another set of relationships within the given social system."[7]

The goal of Padilla is absolutely right. But his seeming refusal to meet people at the point of their own understanding, language and culture *at the outset of the effort,* seems brittle and unrealistic in the multicultural setting found in Los Angeles (where more than 70 languages are spoken in the public schools) and in many, many other cities in our world!

Two Blindnesses

There are two areas of blindness of which Christians must be ever aware. Both are limiting and destructive.

The first is *people* blindness. A failure to see peoples as they are. To recognize that culture is for each person a total thing. Its foods, its values, its language, its little ways of doing things are all bound up together.

Part of our problem with the homogeneous principle is that too many of us unthinkingly bought into the American idea of "the melting pot." The term itself came from a play by Israel Zangwill in 1908 which called America "God's Crucible, the great Melting Pot, where all the races of Europe are melting and reforming!" The play's hero cries, "Germans, Frenchmen, Irishmen and Englishmen, Jews and Russians—into the crucible with you all! God is making the American."[8]

Henry Ford set up a school for his immigrant workers to remake them into our own mold. He taught them English and "made Americans" of them. The graduation exercises featured a huge melting pot on stage into which the graduates marched, wearing their native garb, carrying suitcases. Teachers stirred the contents with huge ladles. Out of the pot on the other side they marched, dressed in "American clothes" and each carrying a little American flag.[9]

We had Scripture to back us up. After all, did not God's Word say that he had made us all one (John 17:11)? That in Jesus Christ we were no longer Jew nor Greek (Galatians 3:28; Colossians 3:11; Romans 10:12)?

And that dream, of everyone coming one day to be like us, dress like us, look like us, speak like us, eat like us, accept Jesus as we have accepted him, a white, fair-haired Jesus as Sallman revealed him—that dream still persists.

People blindness: "When you have seen one you have seen them all."

A Spanish-speaking pastor who fled from Cuba under Batista held services in our Panorama church. He believed that because he spoke Spanish he would eventually be able to attract large numbers of Mexicans who lived in our area. It was highly unlikely. The gospel of Jesus had transcended the political barriers. In his congregation were also people who fled Cuba from Castro. They were united in a faith stronger than political differences. But the gap between the cultures of Cuba and Mexico proved to be too great.

We have been acknowledging the truth of this for a long time. When Stover Kulp first went to Nigeria, West Africa, for the Church of the Brethren in 1922, one of the first things he did was to begin to give those people their own written language. He sensed that they needed to receive the gospel in their own mother tongue. The language in which they made love and made war—their heart language.

And it goes on to this day. Wycliffe Bible Translators have faced death itself to reach tribespeople, teach them how to read and write in their own language, and present them with a New Testament printed in their native tongue.

One translator put the challenge this way. Flipping through the pages of a Bible, an ancient member of the Cakchiquel tribe blurted, "You say this is God's Word, señor, but if your God is so great, why can't he talk in Cakchiquel (a minority tongue spoken by 250,000 Indians)?"

On the spot that missionary decided to give God another tongue, little realizing that he would be devoting the rest of his life to the work.[10]

The problem is becoming more evident in our own land with the change of immigration patterns. In the period 1820-1860, 95% of the immigrants who came to our shores were from Northern and Western Europe. In the period 1971-1974, it had fallen to 6%. The large bulk now come from Asia and Latin America.[11]

The 1980 census proclaims Los Angeles a "minority city," with 48 percent of its population white.[12] By 1990, California is expected to be a "third world" state.[13] The mission field has come to us.

Our communities are changing. Unless Christ is to be

"Do you realize that, with the exception of us, the WHOLE WORLD is made up of FOREIGN COUNTRIES?"

kept exclusively for white, English-speaking peoples, we must learn to share the gospel in the language of the growing masses around us. A Baptist pastor in Glendale, California, says that when he and his people go door to door in their neighborhood, only one family in five speaks English.

The same concern may apply even to some who speak English in our country. Blacks, for example, face language problems. After years of controversy, linguists and educators have come to agree that "a separate black vernacular exists, a language inherently as sound as standard English, but different enough to handicap blacks who use it." They call it "black English" or, in the Los Angeles school district, "Ebonics."[14] Language is one of the barriers some face as they seek to understand the gospel.

People blindness: The failure to see that Jesus was not a white Westerner with blue eyes, wearing a business suit. We have interpreted him in terms of a cultural package which gives him entrance into *our* lives. But are we willing to do this now for others?

The New Testament speaks dramatically to this. The apostle Paul was under fire for becoming as a Gentile when he went to the Gentiles so that he might by "all means" win some (1 Corinthians 9:19-21). He refused to let Jewish Christians force non-Jews into their Jewish cultural mold before they could come to the Christ.

The story of Pentecost is a wonderful example of the God who comes to us *in our own language.* Acts describes that explosive event by saying that people were struck with amazement and wonder. "These people who are talking like this are Galileans! How is it, then, that all of us hear them speaking in our own native languages?" (Acts 2:8, TEV).

A God who comes to us. First by becoming flesh and dwelling among us. By suffering and struggling and by being tempted at every point as we are (Hebrews 4:15). But more than that, by speaking to us in the heart language we understand, in ways that we are best prepared to hear.

People blindness.

But there is a *second* kind of blindness which afflicts us: *kingdom* blindness. Not only must we see the richness of cultural diversity, we must know that God wants his people drawn together into his own family, brothers and sisters together.

We see the breakthrough in the New Testament. First, the eleven disciples were Galileans. So obvious was this that a little slave girl said to a denying Simon Peter in the garden when Jesus was on trial, "You *are* one of them.... Your accent betrays you" (Matthew 26:73, RSV).

In Acts, it was still Galileans. "Men of Galilee, why do you stand looking into heaven?" the voice asks them (Acts

1:11, RSV). At Pentecost it was still Galileans. "Are not all these ... Galileans?" (Acts 2:7, RSV). But a breakthrough began. Not to Gentiles yet. At this point it was to other Jews—Jews from across the known world (Acts 2:9-11). Hellenist Jews.

We see in the pages of the New Testament the tensions over groups. In the early church "the Hellenists murmured against the Hebrews" (Acts 6:1, RSV). When the early church leaders refused to get involved in the deep feelings between the Christians from Jerusalem who were cared for and those who came from other areas to Jerusalem for retirement, but were without care, the office of deacon was created.

The Talmud suggests some 480 synagogues along lines of national or regional origin.[15]

The breakthroughs continue in Acts 11, as verses 20 and 21 have them speaking to the Greeks. The result was that "a great number that believed turned to the Lord."

Clearly the gospel was never intended to be kept for "our kind of people." It is to be shared, to the ends of the earth.

But how?

One illustration of the two blindnesses at work and how to meet them occurs along the Chilean border in Argentina. Baptist churches are located along that border. Every day workers from Chile come across the border to work in Argentina. In many ways the people seem the same. They dress the same, speak the same language, look the same.

Those Argentine churches invited the Chilean workers into their churches, but without success. The workers from Chile felt ill at ease, not at home. The Baptist churches, not discouraged, began Sunday schools for the Chileans. They came. And they came in numbers.

This met the part about *people* blindness. They recognized that there were differences which tended to hold those people at arm's length. But to bear witness to their

PEOPLE / KINGDOM
BLINDNESS / BLINDNESS

oneness in Christ, to the *kingdom* blindness part, they determined that periodically those from Chile and those from Argentina would come together for shared worship.

We do this with our Korean churches. We now share with a Korean church at Glendale also. We come together periodically. We sing the hymns together—they in Korean and we in English. We read the Scripture one verse at a time, in one language, then the other. We offer prayers in each language. The sermon is preached a sentence at a time in one language, then the other.

We have shared in Vacation Bible School together. Once children enter the public schools they lose their former languages and most become fluent in English. We have Korean and "American" (as the Koreans call them) teachers side-by-side, and Korean and American students side-by-side.

Two times a week, I have been attending a class to learn the Korean language. I want to do my part to reach out all the way to them.

Now we are working at combined Sunday schools at both of the churches I serve. But it will be necessary to have some classes in Korean only for those who speak only Korean.

At Panorama City, a family from India has been active in our church. They are working to develop a fellowship of those who want to worship in Gujarati, the language they know the best and with which they feel comfortable.

A Baptist church in downtown Los Angeles—Temple Baptist—had five cultural and language groups worshiping in rooms around a central room. Their services met their cultural understanding and needs. But once a month the walls were removed and they had what they called "sounds of heaven" as they worshiped together.

Another Los Angeles Baptist church—First Baptist— had simultaneous translations in two other languages of the same service—Korean and Spanish. In its Sunday school, children of many languages sat together and seemingly learned together, even though they did not speak the same language. They had some activities together and others by cultural groups. On their staff were persons of various backgrounds.

The patterns may vary, but somehow caring Christians

will put aside the old "melting pot" attitudes and come to see the beauty in each people, each culture.

It is important that we realize that the *key* to McGavran's observation is in the phrase "like to *become* Christians." It was not the end result that he was describing, but the beginning point. Just as Jesus didn't start by laying the Gentile question on Peter. He started by saying to Peter, "Come walk with me. Go with me and learn." Peter came to know more and more what that meant. Even blue-collar, redneck Peter came to begin to sort out what was cultural and what was Christian. But it took some time, some growing.

And it is the Christ who alone can bring us together.

Some years ago, George Webber directed East Harlem Parish. The men of an upper-class, all-white suburban church invited the relatively poor, black men of the East Harlem Parish to a church supper. The men from the comfortable white suburb thought and thought. What could they find in common with the men in the city from Harlem? What could the two groups possibly talk about? The two were completely different in background and outlook. What kind of program could they share?

Someone in the suburban congregation received an inspired idea. No, they would not try to sing so-called fun songs. No, they would not try to manufacture fellowship with games. No, they would not seek some harmless general meeting ground such as sports. They would not discuss economics or politics. On that evening together, they simply went around the circle and asked each man present, black or white, rich or poor, to tell in his own words his response to one question: How had he become a Christian?

That was the reason for their being together. That was the basis for their fellowship. Needless to say, the meeting was one of the most profoundly meaningful any of those men ever attended.

We need to see people in their richness and in the richness of their culture. We need also, at the same time, to see God's dream that we are all his children. Until we see and understand *both* those truths, we have missed a major part of what the gospel declares.

Only the Surface

The fuss over McGavran's formulation has prevented the antagonists from looking at the principle as it is applied in specific situations. Beyond the basic principle are many insights which can help us in reaching various peoples. People within a culture are rated as to the amount of assimilation they have already experienced. C_1 s are those who strongly resist assimilation and cling to their own cultural patterns. C_2 s are those who are partially assimilated. In the United States, they may work at white jobs, speak perfect English, and dress like the prevailing culture. But in their own homes they return to the culture they love and with which they still identify. They live, as it were, in two worlds.

W. E. B. DuBois in *Souls of Black Folk*, published in 1903, described the "double consciousness" constantly experienced by many American blacks. "One ever feels his twoness—an American, a Negro," he wrote. "Two souls, two thoughts, two unreconciled strivings; two warring ideas in one dark body, whose dogged strength alone keeps it from being torn asunder."[16]

DuBois, who helped found the National Association for the Advancement of Colored People, was describing the feelings of blacks whom Church Growth experts would label as C_2 s.

C_3 s are those who have become almost completely assimilated by the prevailing culture. Blacks call them "Oreos." Indians use the term "apples." Asians talk of "bananas." Black or red or yellow on the outside but white on the inside.

Black churches in our country for the most part are made up of C_2 s. They are blacks who move in and out of the white world but still hold strongly to black feelings. C_3s who are Christian are largely in white churches. Most C_1s have not been reached by the Christian faith. It is estimated that there are five million non-Christian blacks in this category in the U.S. How will they be reached? Not by black C_2s. First attempts might be made by black missionaries from African Independent Churches, from some of the 8,000 denominations started as a reaction *against* mission churches. They might come bringing their African robes and banners and drums. Many whites and black C_3s and C_2s would undoubtedly oppose them as "heretics, given to animism and syncretism."

Beneath the Surface

And there is more still about which you need to be aware, at least. Because peoples are nearer or further from us by culture and language, the kind of *evangelism* used will vary, the strategy will be different. Church Growth students have attempted to identify various kinds of evangelism.

Ralph Winter, with the U.S. Center for World Mission, estimates that there are 1,000 million inactive Christians in the world[17]—people who are culturally within the Christian tradition but hardly qualify as committed Christians. They need *renewal* by way of an inner mission or what Church Growth experts call E_0 evangelism. The zero is used because there is no cultural barrier to their vital participation in the life of the church.

Most evangelism and mission effort today has become focused on these groups. In India one report has it as high as 98 percent.

In addition, says Winter, there are 500 million *culturally near* non-Christians. Their cultural tradition and social sphere have already been penetrated by the Christian faith. There already exists some Christian congregation or denomination where they can readily fit in linguistically and socially. E_1 evangelism is the term applied to efforts that must reach across one barrier.

But there are in our world some 2,500 million *culturally distant* non-Christians. Hidden people. Individuals and groups who may live not far away from Christian groups but who are sufficiently different in language and customs, economics, or culture that it simply is not realistic to expect large numbers entering the *geographically close* but *culturally distant* existing Christian churches.

One example is the 97 percent Muslim population of Pakistan which is isolated from the Christian communities of Hindu background in that country. In Acts we read of "the devout persons." As Greeks they did not fit well into the Jewish synagogues Paul visited. E_2 evangelism, unlike E_1 efforts, cannot depend on existing congregations but must create new congregations. E_2 refers to evangelism in a similar (but not the same) culture. The term E_3 is applied to peoples of yet another group—those of a *very different culture.*

Still More

What we have been talking about slices yet another way. The Glenmary Research Center has produced a map of the United States[18] that is colored to show the predominant denomination in each county. Across the deep South you see bright pink indicating Southern Baptists. In areas of Minnesota and Wisconsin orange indicates strong Lutheran membership. In the Northeast and Southwest and at the tip of Texas and the tip of Florida is blue, indicating Roman Catholic (although very different types of Catholic churches in terms of culture and emphasis). Across much of the middle of the country is green, indicating many Methodists. Here and there are yellow counties representing very large percentages of Presbyterians. Other isolated counties indicate a majority of Episcopalians or UCCs. Some are divided, with alternating stripes of two colors. Utah is solid gray, indicating Mormons.

Why is it that no denomination is truly nationwide, coast-to-coast? Some businesses seem to do it. McDonalds seems to be everywhere. Sears. Chevrolet. But not churches.

What sells in Des Moines should sell in San Diego, right? "We are one nation. Indivisible." Some people whose jobs take them to large cities say that the heart of every big city is the same in our great land.

An editor for the *Washington Post* wrote an article a few years ago that has been reprinted in a number of newspapers across the U.S. and in Canada. Later it was expanded into a book, *The Nine Nations of North America.*[19]

His thesis was that we are not one nation, but a *series* of "nations" which cut across state and even national lines into Canada and into Mexico. These nine sections of our continent have "different values, different senses of the pace at which life should be lived, different attitudes about art, food, and ethnic origin, different relationships to nature."[20]

They worship "different gods," he insisted.[21]

No wonder a denomination which takes root and flourishes in one part of the country comes across small and struggling in another part! A new "language," a different style, a totally different feeling tone is needed to "make it" in another of the "nine nations."

Church leaders who want to see the church grow would do well to get a feel for the culture of Dixie, or what the author, Joel Garreau, labels "The Islands," the Foundry, the Breadbasket, MexAmerica, "the Empty Quarter," or New England.

There is no Midwest. "Chicago is an important border metropolis directing the trade in values and enterprise between the Foundry and the Breadbasket."[22]

Any serious student of Church Growth finds that each day new applications of the basic principles become apparent. The morning paper is seen in a totally different light. The movements of peoples, the struggles of the church around the world, the insights of business and industry come to be seen as providing rich raw material to feed the growing understanding of the gospel and to provide insights as to how best it may be shared.

The Task

Far more important than the countless hours spent on arguing over a homogeneous principle is the development of important clues which we need if we are to be serious about the task at hand. The question, suggests Ralph Winter, "is *really very different from what some people see as a tension between social action and evangelism*"[23] (italics his). The more important question is that the focus has shifted for virtually all mainline denominational boards, for "faith missions," and virtually everything in between. No longer is the motivating factor the great commission. Whether it is the United Methodist Church or Sudan Interior Mission, the emphasis, insists Winter, has shifted to the care and feeding of *existing Christian communities.* We have lost sight of mission and have become involved almost exclusively in "interchurch aid." On the other hand, says Winter, "no one has invented a better mechanism for penetrating new social units than the traditional mission society, whether it be Western, African or Asian, whether it be denominational or interdenominational." There is a big job to do, and *we* are uniquely fitted to do it.

This brings us back to McGavran's initial premise. We must make certain that we are aware of the *twin* blindnesses: people blindness and kingdom blindness. But we must soon move beyond all that to the tremendous task of reaching 2,500 million hidden people. Lost, hurting, blind, groping, hungry people.

Donald McGavran in his mid-eighties wrote one book per year while teaching a full load at the School of World Mission at Fuller Seminary.

One of the exciting ones is his book studying this issue

in the context of India, where he spent so many years as a missionary. The book is an excellent resource helping us to see the validity of the approach without our own baggage of feelings about minorities and struggles here which may make us defensive or blur our vision.

McGavran states the challenge so well, as indeed he can. He writes in his book *Ethnic Realities and the Church: Lessons from India,* "The tribes of India are on the march. They will become Marxists, Hindus, Christians, or simple materialists; they will not remain animists. Thousands of missionaries are called for."[24]

The peoples of the world will not remain as they are. We delude ourselves if we sit back saying we don't want to tamper with another's faith. Faith perspectives are changing. Massive winds of change are blowing. If we believe that Jesus indeed brought good news, the keys to life and fulfillment, then we had best open our eyes to the vast shifts. We had better sharpen our own vision to see the differences. We need to use our best thinking to understand the vast differences which must be addressed with skill and creative imagination. A world and its future is in the balance.

Change is all about us. God has called us to be change agents in explosive situations where the stakes are very high.

'I Don't Believe in Numbers'

One of the hesitations people have about Church Growth is in the area of "numbers." "We don't want to get caught up in the numbers game." "We don't want to begin to see people as 'targets' or 'objects' rather than as the focus of love and concern."

It helps, I think, to take a step back and ask, "What is Church Growth?" Peter Wagner answered that in a group discussion recorded in *Leadership* magazine by saying that in the book of Acts Church Growth meant first, *to grow up.* To grow up into Christ (Acts 2:42). To mature in the faith. That is one part of church growth.

Second, in Acts, it meant to *grow together.* To grow in love and concern for each other. Daily they attended the temple together and broke bread in their homes (Acts 2:46).

Third, church growth in Acts meant to *grow out.* To reach out to all who were in need (Acts 2:45). But finally, church growth meant for them to *grow in numbers* (Acts 2:49).[1]

Numbers matter. Numbers mattered to the early church.

I think we have it backwards. Many churches are flooded with pages of numbers regarding *finances.* Hardly a board or committee meets without financial numbers. But we shy away from numbers about *people.* Dollars, yes;

people, no. But a church is in trouble until "people numbers" are as important as "money numbers."

We must first acknowledge, however, that *sometimes there must be less before there can be more.* Sometimes a church must lose people before it can get its act together to move ahead.

Clarence Jordan used to tell of a traveler in the Deep South who came across an integrated church. "How did you ever do it?" the visitor asked. The pastor of the group replied, "I preached them down to two and then we began to grow."

We all know situations that will never grow until the power grip of one or a few persons is broken. Sometimes this must wait for death. Sometimes it comes in other ways.

There is a church in the Midwest which was "blessed" with a talented member who tried to manage everything the church did. One time in a flurry of anger, she and her family walked out and joined another congregation. The first Sunday she was absent, six families that had not been present for a long time returned to the church ... and stayed. Several years later, the church had a revival service. The domineering woman had a beautiful voice and was asked to sing a solo one evening. The evening she sang, not a single person who had been a member when she was a part of the church showed up. The only people present were those who had come into the church after she had left, people who did not know her.

Sometimes there must be less before there can be more.

I once visited a beautiful little Presbyterian congregation. It had been up to 300 or more in attendance not too long before. But during the turbulent sixties, attendance dwindled down to about 100. Those who faithfully came were primarily older, long-term members. Many sat back under the balcony. It was satisfying to sit in that lovely sanctuary, to see the stained glass which portrayed memories out of the past. To sit under the balcony, especially, was to feel almost that you were sitting in a cave. They had traveled across a busy city. Life outside had changed. People of other national backgrounds were moving in. Their area was in marked transition. But there in the sanctuary was security and nourishment. A recalling of a precious past.

I asked Carl George, a Church Growth expert who was with us, what he would do if he were pastor of that church.

"I would not make any changes in the sanctuary," he re-

WHAT WAS DONE IN THE PAST?

plied. "I would not disturb their security. But I would begin to gather other groups together. They might have most of their meetings outside the church. It would take some time until there are several other groups and enough people to challenge those holding on. Until there are enough to not only bring enthusiasm and vision but enough votes to be able to initiate change, nothing will happen. It must be more than one additional group. If it is only one, the old-timers will fight them. If there are several new groups, they can bring the change about."

Carl George's observation is that a congregation cannot double in size without disrupting the power structures. Some key leaders may leave.

I cherish a relationship with one young couple who came to the first church I served. They came out of a Pentecostal background. He kept saying to me, "You need a 'back door' revival. You need to preach some of these people out of the church before it will ever be ready to move ahead."

Sometimes there must be less before there can be more.

There is something sad about a church that never grows.

I returned to a church of my childhood. My father had pastored there. It was a beautiful church, built during the Depression at great cost to the members. Many had mortgaged their own homes to save their church building.

It had wonderful people. Saints of God were among its members. It had had good pastors across the years. Dedicated, able persons had served it.

But as I stood in the pulpit and looked out across the audience almost all of the faces were familiar—even though I had been away for twenty years. Most of the youth who had been my age had moved away. But the saints when I had been there were the same saints, 20 years older now.

The community had grown and changed. A new junior college was not far away. New businesses and new people had moved in around them. A ski lift had been built on the mountains not far away. There were many young couples. But none of this was reflected in the church.

Those people had so much to share. A faith so rich. Lives so grand. But they had maintained the beauty of their fellowship while the world swept on by around them.

There is an old hymn comparing the church to a casket—a jewel box full of gems. That is the picture of the church. Rich treasures. Boxed away and safe.

George Hunter of the United Methodist Church has said we are no longer "fishers of men." We have become "keepers of the aquarium." Someone added that the only way we change the stock of fish is by taking fish from another aquarium.

Recently I traveled in a community with one of the long-term members of a Presbyterian church, listening to what he had to say about his community, and listening more to what he left unsaid. I noted that he talked in terms of the United Presbyterians who might move to his area. There was no Presbyterian church immediately to the north, so he felt they had opportunity for growth.

Some others have set out deliberately to grow by reaching the unchurched. By touching the lives of those outside the church. But some of the rest of us think only in terms of gathering in those of our own faith family who may move nearby. Reaching out is not a part of our understanding.

Many in our day have become *closet Christians.* Ashamed to declare our faith, our allegiance. Strangely silent about our Lord. It isn't really numbers that frightens us. It is an aggressive faith-sharing that causes us to back off. Yet without goals, nothing happens. Without goals we do not act. We are acted upon.

While some churches place a false importance on numbers alone, we must always remember that numbers represent *people.* And our fear of numbers may simply signal a lack of concern for people—God's children.

The truth is, we do share what we have.

A very neat, fastidious bachelor was a guest in the home of some married friends with small children. The couple's little girl climbed up on his knee and said, "Guess what I just got."

He guessed. "A doll?"

"Nope," she said smartly.

"A new dress."

"Nope."

"A new pair of shoes."

"Nope."

"What, then? I give up."

"Chicken pox," she replied, planting a wet kiss on his cheek. And off she went to play.

We do share what we have.

The Christian faith is like chicken pox. If we have it, we share it. We can't help ourselves.

We do talk about what is important to us. We share whatever message we have.

I enjoy looking at California license plates and then, whenever possible, getting a look at the driver. Some plates tell what people do. "I INSURE," announced the owner of a current model Chrysler. One recently had the letters, "BUSY MOM." But the woman inside looked more like a warden from a women's prison. One young woman minus a Dolly Parton wig proclaimed, "IMA925R."

Some tell their mood. One car driven by a young woman was lettered "SHY GAL." One read, "I EXIST." Somebody trying to appear naughty announced, "I GO BARE." But the driver didn't look like someone anyone would want to see bare. Another advertised to all the world, "TENSE." A man in an older car told God and everybody else, "IM AA." Some give their names, "KIM WARD" or "I BONNIE." In the lot in front of the Sheraton Universal Hotel at Universal Studios cars were often seen with plates "EVEL I" and "EVEL II." Behind Dodger stadium in one of the reserved lots during every home game was a red Jaguar: "GARVE

6." (The number 6 was Steve Garvey's Dodger baseball uniform number.)

Many people intend to let others know much about themselves. The owner of a camper went to the expense of acquiring three plates. The first and third had only three letters. Together they said,

SQU	ARE DAN	CER

A rather ordinary young woman with too much makeup announced, "IM A QT." An older man proclaimed, "FOXY POP." A blond in a Honda Accord had the title "BUT CUTE." I tried to supply the beginning: "What" but cute? *Blond* but cute? Or, *dumb* blond but cute? Or what?

A woman I once knew was divorced. With three children, her home had a constant traffic of high school youngsters while she was at work. They smoked pot and drank. Both boys and girls were in and out—anywhere from three to ten of them every school day. Some were there almost all day long. The car out front—a big expensive one—had a license plate that read, "FOR LULU." It was a gift from her married boss. She spent a lot of time doing favors for him in exchange for roses and chocolates and a Cadillac to drive. Some mornings she was just getting home as her children were leaving for school.

A battered station wagon had the identification on its plates, "KIDS CAR." It looked like it had transported more than its share of Little Leaguers and dens of Cub Scouts. It, too, identified the self-image of the mother who drove it.

A black-haired, olive-skinned girl drove a sporty yellow Mercedes with a plate which read simply, "JUDAH."[2]

We do share our message. Given half a chance, we share with all around us, even with strangers, what matters most to us. Part of why we haven't shared more of the gospel with others is that it may not be the most important thing in our lives.

I recall an interdenominational gathering. Standing by

the book display was a leader in another denomination. He was filled with enthusiasm. He bubbled forth, "You have got to read what I think is one of the most exciting new books I have seen in a long time! It is a simply great.' He reached across and lifted up a book on how to insulate your church as a response to the energy crisis.

Now the energy crisis is important. But if how to insulate in the face of that crisis is the most important news we have for our day, somewhere we have gotten off track.

We do share our message, whatever it is. What matters most to us does find its way to our lips and is expressed daily, moment by moment, in our lives.

But we have a more *important* message to share. People are hurting. People are lonely. People are afraid, lost, groping, dying. And we have news too good to hoard.

Sometimes I think that those with the most to share do the poorest job of sharing it.

A mother was asked what position her son played on the high school football team. He was a star but she knew absolutely nothing about football. "I'm not sure," she said, "but I think he is called a drawback."

We have the richest news in all of history. But we handle it so clumsily—or not at all. Sometimes those with the poorest perception of the rich truth (from my biased viewpoint) share it most fervently.

A politician, a priest, the world's smartest man, and a hippie were in an airplane with four parachutes. When the engines failed, the pilot bailed out with the first chute.

The politician took the second one, saying, "I must survive to lead the people."

The world's smartest man jumped out saying, "Without me the world will live in ignorance."

The priest said to the hippie, "Take the last parachute, my son. I am prepared to die."

"That won't be necessary, Father," replied the hippie. "There are two left. The world's smartest man took my knapsack."

Why is it, Jesus asked, that the children of this world are so much wiser in their own generation than the children of light (Luke 16:8)? Why is it that giant denominations with brilliant men and women in leadership, magnificent offices, and the latest in equipment know so much about managing portfolios of finance? They seek out the best professional advice on investment and legal matters. They choose the best architects when building. They consult city planners and reams of statistics about population trends before relocating a church building. Yet when it comes to the great commission, they have no plans, no strategy, no direction, and sometimes even less feeling.

Robert Schuller at the Crystal Cathedral in Anaheim started with nothing and used his unique business, sales, and theological skills to help create a congregation that leaves even some of the cathedrals of Europe small in comparison. Other church people love to jab at him, sometimes with justification, perhaps. But he says it so well, "When we fail to plan, we plan to fail."[3]

On Target

J. Robertson McQuilkin, in his perceptive *Measuring the Church Growth Movement,* asserts boldly that in its insistence on the importance of numbers, "The Church Growth Movement is directly on target." Despite objections from many quarters, "numerical church growth is indeed a crucial task in mission, including the number of people coming into the church and the number of churches constantly increasing." This emphasis has refocused the church's attention on evangelism. He goes on to say, "This is the greatest contribution the Church Growth Movement has made, bringing into sharp focus the issue of the mission of the church. The evidence also indicates that the movement has been very successful, probably the greatest influence in our day in causing many in the world of mission to reaffirm this basic biblical truth."[4]

Numbers Help Us

Numbers matter. We know that when it comes to a pension plan or the denomination's investments. We know that in every other area of life. In business and industry, in education and science and medicine, we know the importance of numbers. We use numbers for measurement and evaluation. We measure quality by quantity.

I recall my high school typing class. The teacher had a reputation for being mean. She would patrol the aisles between the typewriters with a ruler in her hand. She expected us to sit straight, with backs away from the backs of the chair. Both feet flat on the floor in front of us. Fingers curled. Hands above (never resting) on the typewriter. When we forgot, she was not unwilling to crack our knuckles with her speedy ruler.

The day before a speed test she would tell us, "Now tomorrow we have a speed test. Be in bed by nine o'clock tonight. If you aren't, it will show up on the test."

People grumbled. Or laughed. Always behind her back and out of the range of her hearing.

But she was right! My own test scores would be a good 10 to 20 words less when I had been up late the night before. Or when I had skipped breakfast.

We tell ourselves we will scrounge up extra effort, that the best races are run when people are physically tired but mentally alert. But with typing, it did not turn out that

way. Hard cold numbers revealed my bedtime hour the night before.

In virtually every area of life we use numbers to evaluate. We depend on them. And we had better learn that numbers matter with regard to God's most priceless resource—people.

In a recent convention of atomic scientists in Las Vegas, several physicists were spending most of their time around the gambling tables. One tourist exclaimed, "Those scientists are gambling like there is no tomorrow!"

"Maybe they know something," mused an onlooker.

Our world is on a collision course with war and destruction. We have too much to share to simply sit on it. There are far too many reasons why we must be about our Father's business. Our excuses simply do not hold water.

The truth is, *we do believe in numbers.* It may be that it is our faith in the *gospel* that has experienced some slippage.

The bad news in chapter 5 is that turnaround is not easy. If you've been in bed for three weeks with a major illness, it takes tremendous effort and facing a major amount of discouragement to begin to move from that bed and resume an active life again.

The good news is that *it is happening*—in congregations that were as good as dead, in whole judicatories where leadership has a vision, and in a few major denominations.

In my own denomination in California I can point to graphs and show you which congregations have begun to look at the great commission with renewed seriousness! Congregations large or small, urban or rural, liberal or conservative—those which belittled church growth continue to experience marked slippage. But you can *see* which ones have taken it seriously! Their losses have bottomed out. In some cases remarkable growth is beginning to take place!

Where there is no vision a people perish. Where there is

vision and preparation and planning, good things result. God blesses the efforts of the faithful worker. His power is great enough to accomplish his purposes no matter what the odds.

One denomination to watch, we have indicated, is the huge United Methodist Church. The watching game will be fascinating. But even more exciting is playing the game ourselves where we are, among the congregation of God where we live and work.

Networks

A college student was frustrated and angry. She had been assigned a long book to read. After a few pages she could see nothing of worth in it. It was slow reading, poorly written, and about a subject that did not interest her in the least. Boring, boring, boring.

The author, who happened to be another member of the faculty at that school, attended a social gathering at which the student was also present. She met him. He was young, handsome, and engaging—a wonderful conversationalist with exciting ideas.

That night when she was back in her room she picked up the book he had authored. She began to read. To her surprise it suddenly seemed exciting, very readable, something she could not put down. For her the word had become flesh. A warm, personable human being had brought dry words to life.

Dr. Lee Tai-young was the first woman attorney in nearly five thousand years of Korean history. In 1956 she founded a legal aid society for women. In 1970 she founded a Korean branch of the League of Women Voters. In 1971, she received the World Peace Through Law award for her unique contribution to Korean womanhood and human rights.

She gave leadership in building a legal aid center for women. Women in need were drawn to her and she to them. These were women denied their rights by law, women who could not hold property, women who could not keep their children in the event of divorce. Often they were battered wives, women emotionally crushed and spiritually hungry.

Women raised $200,000 of the amount needed for the six-story legal aid center. A lot was purchased on Yoi Island, where the new federal buildings stand and where Republic of Korea troops are reviewed.

But Dr. Lee and her husband were arrested for signing a declaration of human rights on the anniversary of Korea's freedom from the rule of Japan. She was banned from her new law center and was denied her civil rights.

So she gathered small trees and plants from her own yard and those of friends and crossed the bridge to the island on which the center stands and planted the foliage that now beautifies the land around the building.

Still there was a part of her that could not stay away from that place. That building had become her life.

When the scrub woman quit, Dr. Lee reentered the doors to become the scrub woman. On all fours, she lovingly scoured the floors and walls of the center day after day.

There came a time when the women who had worked under her direction could stand it no longer. They came to her and asked her to resume her leadership role. "If they send you to prison, they'll have to send us, too," they promised.

With characteristic courage, Dr. Lee went back to her office, her desk, and her responsibilities. The government tolerated her being there, perhaps feeling she was less of a threat there than someplace else.

Mrs. Lee says, "All of this has been a gift from God. I was involved in too many things; trying to do too much. Now God has permitted me to concentrate on the one thing I consider most important. I can give the rest of my life to the women of Korea."[1]

To countless people in Korea, Dr. Lee Tai-young is "the Word made flesh."

Malcolm Muggeridge wrote about Mother Teresa, "She preaches Christ every moment of every day by living for and in him."[2]

Clarence Jordan, founder of the Koinonia Community, just a few miles out of Plains, Georgia, once said, "How can we evangelize except from the standpoint of incarnation?... Incarnation evangelism is total. It must embrace the whole person. It must not save a soul at the expense of that soul. An evangelism which does not cover the totality of human experience is emasculated and deformed."[3]

The Word must become flesh and dwell among us.

I was returning from a flight to the East Coast, riding on a bus from Los Angeles Airport to the lot near my home where my car was parked. Beside me was an airline employee, a beautiful young woman from El Salvador. She began to talk about her country and her family in El Salvador. How she might never be able to return. About the frequent killings which swept the countryside as the government hunted down critics, many even within the Catholic Church. The next morning, the news item tucked away inside my newspaper took on new meaning. " 'At least 700 people were killed in political violence during the first two weeks of this month, raising this year's political death toll to nearly 9,000,' Roman Catholic officials said Sunday. 'Most of the dead have fallen victim to government troops and right-wing "death squads," ' the officials said."[4]

Because of that young woman from El Salvador, a part of *our world* had become flesh for me in a new way. Awful numbers began to be seen in terms of people!

Body Language

Evangelism is more than reciting short formulas or giving an admonishing word to total strangers. Evangelism comes as one loving heart touches another. As life touches life. It involves more than words. It involves earned trust, strong ties of caring.

A physician friend of mine from Elizabethtown, Pennsylvania, spent a term of service at a mission field in Nigeria, West Africa, with his wife and two small children. Jim and Judith Kipp tried to live on the level of the people. They tried to witness not only with medicine and their lips but by their lifestyle, by the food they grew and what they ate and how they related to each other as a family and to others.

Jim and I reflected on another missionary couple just back from their first term. Roger and Carolyn Schrock and their two small children had gone to the Sudan. They too had tried to live on the level of the people. They built a home like the simple homes there and lived on their food, at their level. The first Sunday Roger and Carolyn were there, they gathered some townspeople under a tree and began services. They had gone to begin work in health care, but their faith went with them.

Jim noted that the added dimension with the Schrocks had been that they were all alone. No other missionary families were there—just Roger and Carolyn and two little children in a strange land and alien culture.

To Africans, Jim noted, life is not divided Western-style into physical, mental, and spiritual. It is all bound together. So when Africans see lives like Roger's and Carolyn's, a tremendous impact is made.

Jim contrasted this with a faith mission in the area which sends a tape recorder and a tape to various tribal chiefs. They listen to the tape. If impressed, they come back to say, "My tribe and I intend to become Christians."

How much deeper the message, the impact, and the change when it comes from flaming lives of love and obvious sacrifice! The gospel is shared most fully by those whose living accompanies their words. God knows we respond most fully when the Word for us becomes flesh.

Christ never calls us to *do* anything or to go anywhere

that he himself would not go. He would never call us to face anything that he has not faced. He would never expect us to love anyone he does not love, or to give anything that he has not given. He himself has set the pattern. And in his own body he has done it all.

The 1981-82 Los Angeles Kings hockey team was probably the one team in the league that had all its teeth. Columnist Jim Murray said they were the kind of fellows you half-expected would cause the organist to strike up "The Dance of the Sugar Plum Fairy" when they skated onto the ice in their gaudy purple and gold uniforms.

Then along came a new coach in mid-season, a fellow named Don Perry. As a player he had his nose broken six times in fights. His scar-tissue face looked like a patient in search of a plastic surgeon.

The players loved him. Mike Murphy, a King longer than anyone on the roster, was filled with emotion when he said the thing he liked is that Perry worked as hard as any of them. He didn't expect any effort of the players that he himself was not willing to give. He said, "This is what you have to do and this is how you do it."[4]

My mind recalled lines from Isaiah 53. "There was nothing attractive about him ... but he endured the suffering that should have been ours" (TEV).

The Christ who gave of himself without limit will himself go with us into the face of any situation, even into the jaws of death itself.

Perhaps nowhere is it put more beautifully than in the great passage in the late Boris Pasternak's *Doctor Zhivago.*

> Rome was a flea market of borrowed gods and conquered peoples, a bargain basement on two floors, earth and heaven, a mass of filth ... eyes sunk in fat, sodomy, double chins, illiterate emperors, fish fed on the flesh of learned slaves ... all crammed into the passages of the Colosseum, and all wretched.

And then, into this tasteless heap of gold and marble *He* came, light and clothed in an aura, emphatically human, deliberately provincial, Galilean, and at that moment gods and nations ceased to be and man came into being—man the carpenter, man the plowman, man the shepherd with his flock of sheep at sunset, man who does not sound in the least proud, man thankfully celebrated in all the cradle songs of mothers and all the picture galleries the world over.[5]

As the apostle Paul wrote to the church at Philippi,

The attitude you should have is the one that Christ Jesus had: He always had the nature of God, but he did not think that by force he should try to become equal with God. Instead of this, of his own free will he gave up all he had, and took the nature of a servant ... and appeared in human likeness. (Philippians 2:5-6, TEV)

God comes to us on our own turf, speaking our language, entering fully into our worlds. As we go to others we can do no less if we would share the riches of the gospel.

Orlando Costas puts it plainly. "The gospel requires a concrete, incarnate witness."[6]

We share the gospel easiest and best with those we know the best.

But we make it so difficult.

With Those You Know and Love the Best

A pastor in a southern California community not far away talked to me about the impossible setting for his congregation. Earlier in his life he had pastored a fast-growing suburban church in Denver. The congregation he was presently serving was made up of wonderful, talented people. But the community was changing. People of other races, other nationalities, and other economic levels were moving in. Try as they would, few of their new neighbors ever darkened their doors.

A black congregation came and asked to share their facilities. The congregation approved this and it became a very satisfying experience. The two congregations shared in many activities, even though their styles of worship were worlds apart.

"But how do we grow?" he asked. "How do we reach the people around us who are so different in almost every respect?"

We make it so difficult.

I tried to say to him, "Start in the ways that are most natural for you." But he did not hear.

All of their members had friends. All of their members had work associates. Many of their members had relatives. All of their members had neighbors. All of them had ties to other people—deep personal ties. If he could only have seen what should have been so obvious. Don't start with total strangers. Start with those you know and love the most!

"But isn't this racist?" some white pastors asked a pastor friend of mine of Mexican descent.

His reply: "It's racist only if all your friends are white."

Existing Networks

There are networks of people across our country.

If someone handed you a letter and said, "Can you get this to the president of Harvard University by using only people who know each other," could you do it? Or a letter to the President of the United States, using a network of people who know other people?

Someone actually tried this in downtown Los Angeles not long ago, handing envelopes to total strangers. It took about five people on the average to get the message through.

We all know people who know people who know someone important.

Our nation is made up of networks. On my block are networks.

Three in my immediate block are Roman Catholics. They have close ties with one another. A black family across the street and two doors down is very friendly. They stop and talk. But their paths do not cross mine. They are Jehovah's Witnesses. Directly across the street is a Mexican-American family. We are "friendly," but not close friends. Across the street two doors down the other way is a family with kids on drugs. They are part of a different network.

Across the street is a formerly inactive Protestant family. They have become our friends and have joined our church. Next door to our left is another inactive Protestant family. They are just starting their family, expecting a child in a month. I know realistically that they are the best prospects for our church. The ties to them are much closer.

The Catholic families are friendly, but their closest ties are to each other. Their children go to the same parochial schools. They have a feeling tone and patterns of living which are different somehow.

Long ago Donald McGavran, the father of the modern Church Growth movement, discovered these networks while serving in India. He wrote a book—the first to introduce his developing ideas about Church Growth—called *Bridges of God*.[7]

We need to use the ties we have, working the networks from those close at hand to those out at the fringes. Robert Schuller at Crystal Cathedral does this very effectively. Serving a blue collar area, he plays to various professional groups which have strong ties to each other.

For example, he works at cultivating members of the police force. Not one by one, but as a group. One of my few times there during the week they were having a funeral for a policeman shot in the course of duty. The lot had more police cars and motorcycles than the police headquarters.

He works at cultivating fire fighters.

I had to think of things that have contributed to growth

in other settings where I have been. In my last church—a college church—an attractive nursery staffed by many from the church drew young couples new to that community into the Sunday school and church as well. A network of young couples with children was effectively worked by that congregation.

That congregation also won its way into the network of high school teachers. The head of the teachers' union was a part of the church. The minister of music had the high school choral music. The church was available to teachers for various activities. At one point the teachers were at odds with the school board over the possible dismissal of older teachers with seniority to cut costs. Three of the members of the school board were members of our congregation, but the church made available a room for the teachers to meet and discuss their concerns. The word spread. Teachers who had felt themselves alienated from the church, having "outgrown" religion, found friends they worked with drawing them back into the life of that church.

Networks.

The most basic network, of course, is the family.

Long ago my dad, serving in industrial Lima, Ohio, during World War II, observed that simply getting children into the Sunday school is not enough. If you do not win the parents also, it will be difficult to hold the children as they grow older.

Donald McGavran discovered this, too. The gospel spreads best not drip by drip, but by what he called *people movements*. Not whole masses being baptized without meaning. But, rather, as groups of individuals together come to decisions and move together into the fold.

In a home, for example (especially in a culture where the man is considered the absolute head), if a wife has received the Christian faith, it is better if she can hold back her decision until the husband and other members of that family come with her. One wife alone faces wither-

PEOPLE MOVEMENTS

WHOLE
VILLAGES

"And all the residents of Lydda and
Sharon . . . turned to the Lord."
Acts 9:35

LARGE
NUMBERS

"Now at Iconium, . . . a great
company believed, both Jews
and Greeks." Acts 14:1

WHOLE
FAMILIES

"Lydia . . . was baptized with her
household." Acts 16:15

ing opposition. But when a family comes together there is mutual support. And the result will be far more firm and lasting.

McGavran makes it clear that he is not advocating mass movements and certainly not a neglect of quality. Rather, "multi-individual, mutually interdependent conversion."[8] McGavran notes that "at least two-thirds of all converts in Asia, Africa and Oceania have come to the Christian faith through people movements."

The chief resistance of Islam and other religions, McGavran argues, is social, not theological. "If social resistance can be overcome, the gospel can be heard."

One by one against a social tide is a slow and painful way to grow. But where families and whole villages hear the word and come to Christ together, there is far less social dislocation and less searing wounds between members of the same family. Normal relationships can remain intact. "People-movement churches are therefore more stable . . . and more likely to bear up under persecution," says McGavran.[9]

What is true overseas is true here to a greater extent than we might imagine.

We have not often thought of discipling a family or a group out to the fringes. We, with our Americanized, frontier-influenced individuality, think of "drip by drip" evangelism, as McGavran calls it. One here. Another there.

The missionaries of the New Testament did not confine their efforts to "drip by drip" evangelism. Its pages are rich in the stories of whole families, and in some instances, entire villages coming to accept Christ.

In a sense, the concept of people movements is simply an application of the homogeneous principle. Jesus used it all the time as we indicated earlier. We see his focus on those who were tied in with the fishing trade. As he approached tax collectors. First one, then a whole roomful. After Jesus talked with the Samaritan woman at the well, she brought her village to meet him (John 4:28-30). The

Gadarene demoniac wanted to go with him when he was delivered. But Jesus instructed him, "Return to your home, and declare how much God has done for you" (Luke 8:39, RSV). We see it among networks of women.

But the early church used it, too. Acts 9:35 speaks of whole villages: "All the residents of Lydda and Sharon . . . turned to the Lord." It tells of large numbers. Acts 14:1 says, "Now at Iconium . . . a great company believed, both Jews and Greeks." And it speaks of whole families coming. Acts 16:15: "Lydia . . . was baptized, with her household." And Acts 16:33: "The jailer . . . was baptized . . . with all his family" (RSV).

A good friend harshly critical of the Church Growth movement asserted, "In all the New Testament writings, only *Luke* was interested in numbers. The others did not care about numbers." The implication was that evangelism and church growth are side issues—not central to the gospel.

The impressive thing to me, however, is to see how all of the church growth principles which are discovered in our day were present all along in the pages of the New Testament.[10] The New Testament has become a whole new book for me. Never again will I be able to read it as I once did. I cannot read its pages without seeing church growth strategy at work. This particular area is one worth exploring for yourself. Reread the stories of the ministry of Jesus and the apostles. Not only in Acts, the little insights keep shining through in the letters as well. Even Revelation, thought by some to be only about last things, teaches us volumes about churches and growth. See for yourself how many of the elements which McGavran and Wagner and others have discovered in our day reveal themselves in the pages of Scripture. And we were too blind to see.

I recently ate lunch with the pastor of a small church that has experienced tremendous growth. When I probed his mind, he shared how much of their growth had come from people with whom the members worked. One worker brought a co-worker and his family. That family brought another.

He himself used the web principle. He told of a 12-year-old boy who was killed when his bike was hit by a car. The boy lived in the same block as the church. The pastor was asked to conduct the funeral. He spent hours with the family.

"I went to every other family connected with the family who lost their son," he told me. "The grandparents. The neighbors. All the friends who came to the funeral. I spent time with all of them. As a result, several of those families found their way into the church."

A 70-some-year-old pastor had built (as a younger man) a congregation in Seattle from a small, ingrown group to a thriving congregation. Weddings, funerals, every service of the church became a prospect list of people to love, care about, and woo. Now retired, he serves a small congregation in Salkum, Washington. When his pastor-son visited him, he found him out to breakfast at 6:00 a.m. with a group of businessmen from that small town.

"What are you doing, Dad?" his son asked.

"I'm just trying to build up community awareness for our church," was his reply.

One of the churches I serve grew the fastest when the pastor's wife was a member of the PTA, played for its programs, and developed music programs for them. The same people were recruited into her church choir. A network of PTA and Little League parents were drawn into the church through the vivacious, talented pastor's wife.

The networks are there—people with their ties to one another. Jesus used them. The apostles Paul and Peter used them. We will, too, if we are serious about sharing our faith.

Responding to Responsiveness

Eric Schubert has important things to teach us. On Saturday, November 2, 1985, Schubert was coaching football at Lakeland Regional High School in Wanaque, New Jersey, which is what he had been doing all season. The next day he kicked five field goals to help the New York Giants to a 22-20 victory over the winless Tampa Bay Buccaneers.

"Last week I was coaching and watching the Giants game on TV. Today I was *on* TV," Schubert said.

Actually, during the summer of 1985, Schubert had tried out to play football with the Giants. In a preseason game one Saturday night, he kicked the winning field goal against the New York Jets. On the very next Monday morning he was cut from the squad.

So Eric Schubert went back to high school coaching.

But suddenly the Giants were in a bind. One of their kickers was on the injured reserve list. Another had been claimed by the St. Louis Cardinals.

Coach Bill Parcells phoned Eric and signed him to play for one game only. Schubert was perfect that day on his field goal attempts of 24, 36, 24, 41, and 33 yards.[1]

The point is that Schubert, earlier rejected, went back to coach high school football. But Eric Schubert was ready! His *foot* was ready! When the door opened and opportunity said, "Go!" he was prepared, and he went.

Jesus had a story about ten attendants at a wedding. The groom did not arrive on time. Five of the young women had their lamps filled with oil. The wicks were trimmed and their lamps were burning. Five of them were not ready. When the groom arrived, those who were ready were invited into the party. Those that were not ready were left out in the cold (Matthew 25:1-13, TEV).

An old Negro spiritual has it "I wanna be ready ... to walk in Jerusalem, just like John."

In space shots, there is a "launch window" into outer space, "a limited opening in terms of both precise time and precise space through which a space shot must pass if it is to be successful."[2]

There come to our lives such *windows of opportunity*. We need to be ready. We need to be prepared mentally, physically, and psychologically when the precise moment comes. When the window passes by, we must move through that window. We must seize our opportunity for action.

After early successes in his attempts at nonviolent resistance to segregation, Martin Luther King, Jr., went to Birmingham, Alabama, which some had called "the most segregated city in the South." King ended up in jail. Eight Alabama clergymen wrote a letter to Martin Luther King saying that he was pressing too hard. They contended that time was needed to heal the injustices. His sense of urgency, they said, was offending moderates and hardening the opposition. They called his actions "unwise and untimely."

King responded on scraps of paper which were smuggled from his cell. It later came to be known as the classic "Letter from a Birmingham Jail."

King answered his pious critics, saying that "time itself is neutral." Time without action does not automatically bring good.

After citing the injustices felt by his people—the murders, the mobs, the cursing and brutalizing they had endured—King quoted a "distinguished jurist of yesterday" who had said that "justice too long delayed is justice denied."[3]

In our lives and in the lives of those about us, there come rare moments which are ripe for action. And it is just as true for us as it was for King: opportunities ignored, action delayed, may mean opportunities lost.

There are moments when people are ready, when the time is ripe. *Good News for Modern Man* says, "When the right time finally came" (Galatians 4:4). Jesus came "in the fullness of time," the *kairos* moment. Many things converged to make it "the right moment."

But that moment also passes. "Once to every man and nation comes the moment to decide," wrote James Russell Lowell concerning the challenges presented at the time of the struggle for an end to slavery in the United States. "And that choice goes by forever 'twixt that darkness and that light."[4]

Receptive Times

Long ago Donald McGavran discovered this in India with regard to reaching people for Christ. There are times when entire peoples are receptive. Sometimes after a war or other hardship. Sometimes when they are dislocated from homeland or life as they had known it.[5]

J. A. Robinson, a pastor of a generation ago, serving in Johnstown, Pennsylvania, during the great Depression, kept careful records and noted that the giving level among that blue-collar group of people in a fairly large congregation was actually higher during the depression when many of them were out of work, scraping to barely make it, than it was either before or after that period. Hard times increased dedication.

The Hebrew people illustrated this again and again. They were seemingly most faithful when times were hard. They seemed most indifferent when life was easier. Many people can survive all kinds of difficulty. Few can survive good times with faith and devotion at a high level.

McGavran discovered that there are receptive times for groups and for individuals.

A youngster of 12 is more open to dedication of life than is a person in the late teens. Most of the tribes and religious groups of the world have discovered this. Bar mitzvah, tribal initiation ceremonies, catechism, and baptism for believers churches usually come at the time of known receptivity rather than later—even though a youth may be more aware of what is taking place later.

In our own communities we see receptive times. Many people are more receptive at time of sickness or in the face of death. Young couples may be more receptive at the time of marriage. Or at the birth of the first child. Or when the first child goes to school and the mother finally is aware that her influence on that child has been severely diminished. Or when the last child leaves home and a sudden harsh loneliness or self-examination sets in. Or at the time of retirement.

Moving to a new community is often a time of receptivity. Old friends are left behind. Old patterns and loyalties are not there. Rootless and friendless, the reshaping of life and interests may be a time of receptivity.

Times of stress

One clue to times of receptiveness is a person's level of stress. Holmes and Rahe ranked stress-causing situations in life and judged the effect of each by number.[6]

To even list these is to call attention to the church's ability or lack of ability to respond to difficult stress periods in lives. Sometimes churches or individuals are so filled with judgment that they are unable to respond to the open doors into hurting people's hearts. Sometimes the hurting people perceive the church as judgmental, even if this is not the case.

Read through Holmes and Rahe's list and note the progression.

Life Event	Mean Value
1. Death of spouse	100
2. Divorce	73
3. Marital separation	65
4. Jail term	63
5. Death of close family member	63
6. Personal injury or illness	53
7. Marriage	50
8. Fired at work	47
9. Marital reconciliation	45
10. Retirement	45
11. Change in health of family member	44
12. Pregnancy	40
13. Sex difficulties	39
14. Gain of new family member	39
15. Business readjustment	39
16. Change in financial state	38
17. Death of close friend	37
18. Change to different line of work	36
19. Change in number of arguments with spouse	35
20. Mortgage over $10,000	31
21. Foreclosure of mortgage or loan	30
22. Change in responsibilities at work	29
23. Son or daughter leaving home	29
24. Trouble with in-laws	29
25. Outstanding personal achievement	28
26. Wife begin or stop work	26
27. Begin or end school	26
28. Change in living conditions	25
29. Revision of personal habits	24
30. Trouble with boss	23
31. Change in work hours or conditions	20
32. Change in residence	20
33. Change in schools	20
34. Change in recreation	19
35. Change in church activities	19
36. Change in social activities	18
37. Mortgage or loan less than $10,000	17
38. Change in sleeping habits	16
39. Change in number of family get-togethers	15

40. Change in eating habits **15**
41. Vacation **13**
42. Christmas **12**
43. Minor violations of the law **11**

(Used by permission of Pergamon Journals, Inc., and Thomas H. Holmes.)

The Institute for American Church Growth has expanded on this. The Holmes-Rahe Stress Scale related primarily to adults. Win Arn in his *Growth Report* suggests lists for preschool, elementary school, junior high, and senior high youth.[7]

Preschool Age

Life Event	Rank
1. Death of a parent	**89**
2. Divorce of parents	**78**
3. Marital separation of parents	**74**
4. Jail sentence of a parent for one year or more	**67**
5. Marriage of a parent to stepparent	**62**
6. Serious illness requiring hospitalization	**59**
7. Death of a brother or sister	**59**
8. Acquiring visible deformity	**52**
9. Serious illness requiring hospitalization of a parent	**51**
10. Birth of a brother or sister	**50**
11. Mother taking job	**47**
12. Increase in arguments between parents	**44**
13. Starting nursery school	**42**
14. Addition of a third adult to family (e.g., grandparent)	**39**
15. Brother or sister leaving home	**39**
16. Having visible congenital deformity	**39**
17. Increase in number of arguments with parents	**39**
18. Change in acceptance by peers	**38**
19. Death of a close friend	**38**
20. Serious illness requiring hospitalization of brother or sister	**37**

Elementary School Age

22. Change in father's occupation requiring
     increased absence from home **45**
23. Mother beginning to work **44**
24. Jail sentence of parent for 30 days or less **44**
25. Serious illness requiring hospitalization
     of brother or sister **41**
26. Addition of third adult to family
     (e.g., grandparents) **41**
27. Outstanding personal achievement **39**
28. Loss of job by parent **38**
29. Death of a grandparent **36**
30. Brother or sister leaving home **36**
31. Pregnancy in unwed teenage sister **36**
32. Change in parents' financial status **29**
33. Beginning another school year **27**
34. Decrease in number of arguments
     with parents **27**
35. Decrease in number of arguments
     between parents **25**
36. Becoming a full-fledged member of a church . . . **25**

Junior High Age

Life Event	Rank
1. Pregnancy out of wedlock	**95**
2. Death of a parent	**94**
3. Divorce of parents	**84**
4. Acquiring a visible deformity	**83**
5. Marital separation of parents	**77**
6. Jail sentence of a parent for one year or more . . .	**76**
7. Male partner in pregnancy out of wedlock	**76**
8. Death of a brother or sister	**71**
9. Having a visible congenital deformity	**70**
10. Discovery of being an adopted child	**70**
11. Becoming involved with drugs or alcohol	**70**
12. Change in child's acceptance with peers	**68**
13. Death of a close friend	**65**
14. Marriage of a parent to stepparent	**63**
15. Failure of a grade in school	**62**
16. Pregnancy in unwed teenage sister	**60**
17. Serious illness requiring hospitalization	**57**

18. Beginning to date **55**
19. Suspension from school **54**
20. Serious illness requiring hospitalization
     of a parent **54**
21. Move to a new school district **52**
22. Jail sentence of a parent for 30 days or less..... **50**
23. Birth of a brother or sister **50**
24. Failure to be accepted in an extracurricular
     activity he or she wanted **48**
25. Loss of job by a parent **48**
26. Increase in number of arguments
     between parents **48**
27. Breaking up with boyfriend or girlfriend...... **47**
28. Increase in number of arguments
     with parents **46**
29. Beginning junior high school **45**
30. Outstanding personal achievement **45**
31. Serious illness requiring hospitalization
     of brother or sister **44**
32. Change in father's occupation requiring
     increased absence from home **42**
33. Change in parents' financial status **40**
34. Mother beginning to work **36**
35. Death of a grandparent...................... **35**
36. Addition of a third adult to family
     (e.g., grandparent)........................ **34**
37. Brother or sister leaving home **33**
38. Decrease in number of arguments
     between parents **29**
39. Decrease in number of arguments
     with parents **29**
40. Becoming a full-fledged member of a church ... **28**

Senior High School Age
Life Event	Rank
1. Getting married	**101**
2. Unwed pregnancy...........................	**92**
3. Death of a parent	**87**
4. Acquiring a visible deformity	**81**
5. Divorce of parents	**77**

6. Male partner in pregnancy out of wedlock......**77**
7. Becoming involved with drugs or alcohol **76**
8. Jail sentence of a parent for one year or more...**75**
9. Marital separation of parents **69**
10. Death of a brother or sister **68**
11. Change in acceptance by peers...............**67**
12. Pregnancy in unwed teenage sister............**64**
13. Discovery of being an adopted child **64**
14. Marriage of a parent to stepparent **63**
15. Death of a close friend **63**
16. Having a visible congenital deformity.........**62**
17. Serious illness requiring hospitalization **58**
18. Failure of grade in school **56**
19. Move to a new school district **56**
20. Failure to be accepted in an extracurricular
activity he or she wanted **55**
21. Serious illness requiring hospitalization
of a parent...............................**55**
22. Jail sentence of a parent for 30 days or less.....**53**
23. Breaking up with a boyfriend or girlfriend **53**
24. Beginning to date...........................**51**
25. Suspension from school **50**
26. Birth of a brother or sister **47**
27. Increase in number of arguments
with parents............................**46**
28. Increase in number of arguments
between parents **46**
29. Loss of job by a parent.......................**46**
30. Outstanding personal achievement **46**
31. Change in parents' financial status **45**
32. Being accepted at a college of his/her choice ...**43**
33. Beginning senior high school **42**
34. Serious illness requiring hospitalization
of brother or sister **41**
35. Change of father's occupation requiring
increased absence from home **38**
36. Brother or sister leaving home **37**
37. Death of a grandparent......................**36**
38. Addition of third adult to family
(e.g., grandparent) **34**

                   (Used by permission of the Institute for American Church Growth.)

If we care about reaching people, we will spend some time with these lists. We will be aware of which changes most produce pressure within people and then be alert and sensitive, tuned into people as these occur.

In time of need, hurting people often reach out. When the circumstances of life disrupt, people are often ready to be touched by a healing hand when otherwise the walls are too high and the interest is simply not there.

Jesus Used Receptiveness

Jesus knew about this. His ministry was almost entirely to hungry people, hurting people, sick and desperate people. Almost never was he able to minister to the spiritually stuffed, the smug, the satisfied. Read it for yourself.

Jesus instructed his disciples to go to those who were receptive. And to bypass temporarily those who were not yet ready. As he sent out twelve disciples, as recorded in Matthew 10, he instructed them not to go among the Gentiles or Samaritans but to go instead to "the lost sheep of the people of Israel."

And he was more specific than that. As they moved among those he perceived to be most receptive at that time, he knew that even among the Jews there would be unreceptive people. Verse 11 of Matthew 10 has him saying, "When you come to a town or village, go in and look for someone who is willing to welcome you." But "if some home or town will not welcome you or listen to you, then leave that place and shake the dust off your feet" (verse 14, TEV).

Invest your energies with those who are receptive.

How this simple awareness could have helped me across my ministry! How many hours I spent on people where the doors of their hearts were closed (at that moment) while I disregarded open doors so close at hand!

The apostle Paul also sensed when doors were closed and when they were open.

Acts 17 talks of Paul and Silas traveling through Amphipolis and Apollonia, coming to Thessalonica, where there was a synagogue. Why? Paul, as always, with so short a time to do so much, invested himself where he thought he had an opening.

Read Acts for yourself and see the principle at work.

And what of resistant peoples? Do you ignore them? Those who have turned their back on the church who seem cold and indifferent?

The advice of Church Growth people is to "hold them lightly." Keep lines of communication open. Let them know you care about them—that the door is always open. But do not pressure. Receptivity will return. At some point in their lives there will be an opening. But not now. Not just yet. Wait for the stirring which will one day come.

In a "Roto-Rooter" ad some years ago a man from that company says, "You don't know me. But one day you will need me."

The church must learn to move in when people are hurting, ready, and hungry. The church must also learn how to wait, to be ready when the "right time" comes.

Receptiveness in the World

What we are talking about is more than common sense or educated hunches. Among serious Church Growth people it may become highly technical.

By using and developing methods of "soil testing," Church Growth students feel they can survey various parts of the world and say with relative certainty, as one man said after study of his native Indonesia, "I can tell you where to go and work for five years with almost no results.

I can also tell you where to go in Indonesia and come back with results."

Since 1979, Peter Wagner and Edward Dayton have edited an annual each year entitled *Unreached Peoples.*[8] It is a joint project of the Strategy Working Group of the Lausanne Committee for World Evangelization and the MARC (Missions Advanced Research and Communication Center) ministry of World Vision International. As it lists the unreached peoples of the world by tribe, language, and nation, it gives an assessment of their openness to change and their receptivity to religion. Groups are indexed by receptivity: very receptive, receptive, indifferent, reluctant, very reluctant, and unknown.

The vocation of mission has become highly sophisticated. There is so much to learn. And so much has already been learned. Still, many sincere Christians, with minds closed firmly against anything that speaks of "Church Growth," have made themselves far poorer by ignoring this knowledge.

We know, for example, that Koreans (for a variety of reasons) are currently especially receptive to the Christian religion.

In Korea following World War I, Christians were at the forefront of a nonviolent movement of noncooperation against the Japanese, seeking to force Japan to grant self-government to Korea. Of the 33 signers of the Korean Declaration of Independence, 15 were Christians, some of them prominent Protestant ministers. The church became the rallying point for the oppressed Korean people. And the church experienced a surge of growth in most provinces.[9]

But in India, Donald McGavran contended that Christians feared a self-governing state of Hindus and Muslims would persecute them. McGavran argues that Christians did not join the fight for freedom in number. Therefore, he feels, nationalism in India retarded the growth of the church.[10]

There are from 16 to 17 million refugees today. Many of them are especially responsive to the gospel. Cambodia has been resistant for years. But Cambodian refugees are especially receptive now. Navajo Indians are especially receptive now. But receptivity passes. It does not last forever.

A story out of the Iranian Hostage Crisis period illustrates this. Three cardinals of the Church of Rome were killed in an auto accident and found themselves face to face with God in heaven. Each was filled with questions. The first cardinal, from Italy, asked, "Tell me, Father, about the future of the church. We are all glad for our Polish pope. But will there ever be an Italian pope again?" God reassured him that in the course of years to come there will be many Italian popes.

The second cardinal, from the United States, asked, "Tell me, will we ever have a pope from America?"

"Yes," said God, "the church has grown strong in the United States. In time you will have a pope from your land."

The third cardinal, from Teheran, asked, "And what about us? I know that things are difficult now. But will there ever be a pope from Iran?"

God thought for a long moment and then replied, "It is certainly possible. But not in *my* lifetime."

The saddest part about the whole Iranian tragedy was that it might never have happened if Christians centuries before had been responsive to responsiveness.

In 1271 there existed the greatest empire the world had ever seen—the empire of the Mongol Kublai Khan. The empire stretched from the Ural Mountains to the Himalayas and from the China Sea to the Danube. Kublai Khan in that year sent Nicolò and Maffeo Polo as his ambassadors to the pope in Rome with a request: "Send me a hundred skilled in your religion ... and so I shall be baptized, and so all my barons and great men, and their subjects. And so there will be more Christians here than there are in all your parts."

A wide-open door for Christ across the entire East! But the pope was too busy playing politics. For 18 long years precisely nothing was done. Not a single missionary was sent. Then, in 1289, a handful were sent. Too few, too late. And the chance was gone.[11]

Think of it! If the church had seized the opportunity in 1271, there might have been no such thing as a "pagan India" or a "Red China" or a "Muslim Iran." There might have been no ayatollas. The East might have been Christian from end to end. What a vision! What a tragedy! What a different world it might have been! Willingness by God's people to respond to an open door back then might have meant no "444 days" of agony and separation in our own day.

There is responsiveness. Sometimes among an entire nation. And then the door swings shut. "And the choice goes by forever," said Lowell.

I think of a dear friend in Harrisburg. I was young in the ministry. He was the executive for the Harrisburg Council of Churches. His name was Joseph Woods, a former Presbyterian missionary to China. One day he shared that one of his students in the mission school had been Chou En Lai, later a leader in China. Chou had been agnostic with regard to religion—young, eager, questioning. Not at all negative, he was willing to learn. But he was not convinced.

Later, as a key statesman in the Red Chinese movement, Chou had pleaded with friends at the American embassy in Peking to be allowed to fly to the United States to visit President Franklin Roosevelt to try to explain the Chinese Revolution to him. He was repeatedly turned down.

In 1954, Chou helped design the Geneva Conference, which temporarily halted the Vietnam fighting. In Geneva shortly afterward, he saw John Foster Dulles, not only a famous statesman but well known as a Presbyterian churchman. As Dulles approached him, Chou courteously extended his hand in friendship to the American Secretary of State.

Dulles refused to shake the outstretched hand, humiliating Chou En Lai in front of the entire gathering. Observers such as Theodore White later remarked that it may have been the "costliest display of rudeness by any diplomat anywhere." Hurt, angry, and humiliated by the deliberate insult, Chou became an unrelenting enemy of American diplomacy for many years.

Doors are open for us—doors of receptiveness which may have been long closed. If we fail to see and respond, long agony and unforeseen consequences may be ours.

Receptiveness Around Us

It is true for wide areas of the world. It is true for nations and groups of people. It is true for individual lives which touch ours.

It comes down to you and me.

When God opens a door, walk through it. Do not hesitate. For that door will not remain open long.

It is a discovery of Church Growth. It was the pattern of Jesus and the early church. It is a fact about the nature of life in God's world.

Trickle-Up Evangelism

Ralph Elliott, in a *Christian Century* article entitled "Dangers of the Church Growth Movement,"[1] made two charges that are especially worth exploring. Elliott spoke of church growth as promoting "a tribal consciousness" whereby "main leaders are captured first for the church, and then everyone else follows."

Trickle-Down Evangelism

Actually, this has sometimes been the approach of the church. In China, some assumed that because Madam Chiang Kai-shek became Christian, all of China was safely tucked away within the Christian fold.

I have heard pastors talk with pride of the number of medical doctors or lawyers or Ph.D.s or school superintendents who are members of their congregation, as if that gives them a special hold on the population.

But the charge that this is the approach of the Church Growth movement is not accurate. This is the opposite of what McGavran observed.

McGavran quoted J. Waskom Pickett who noted that movements to Christ "have not generally developed where missionaries were most widely associated with the government" and hence with rulers of the people, "nor in areas where Western influence has been most strongly felt" through schools and colleges where upper and middle classes were educated.[2]

McGavran noted that Arnold Toynbee "pointed out that, far from a new religion first being accepted by the classes and then by the masses, it is usually first accepted by the proletariat."[3]

"Higher religions," said Toynbee, "make their entry into society from *below upwards* and the dominant minority (the classes) is either unaware of these new religious movements or ... is hostile to them.... In the Roman Empire the *philosophies* appealed to the middle class.... Christianity appealed to the masses."[4] Said McGavran, "When God selected a people in Egypt, and made a covenant with it, he chose not the learned, not the princes, not the aristocrats, not the students—but the slaves."[5]

The Old Testament story is repeated in the New.

> Of the twelve apostles, eleven were Galileans—country people who spoke with an accent. The rulers, elders, scribes and high priests scorned them as "uneducated common men" (Acts 4:13). The Book of Acts tells us that the Christian religion spread through the masses in Jerusalem and Judea. The common people heard the apostles gladly.[6]

Sometimes a mission has failed in its attempt to reach the learned in a society only to find one of its cast-offs begin to preach to a scorned "inferior" tribe nearby with startling results.

McGavran spoke of missionaries who wondered whether they ought to baptize Untouchable converts in India. "Many a missionary," he said, "has remarked, 'I would rather baptize one Brahman than a thousand Chamars [Untouchables].' Whole missions never started work among the depressed, but stressed educational work among the upper castes largely on the grounds that the Depressed Classes were (as the Hindus always declared) inferior peoples who would never make good Christians."[7]

This is hardly the approach of God at work in the Scriptures. McGavran contended in his early work, *The Bridges of God*, "the barbarians, the slaves, the untouchables, the primitives, of today can provide the leaders, of tomorrow."[8]

The Cities and God

Ralph Elliott also charged that church growth "theology" is "dangerous in dooming the city to hopelessness."

Actually McGavran calls cities the *key* to church growth. "Many conditions conducive to church growth are found in cities. Uprooted and transplanted immigrants, starting life anew in strange surrounding, and needing community and friendship, flood into cities. These newcomers are away from the close control of family and intimates."[9]

One cannot read much of McGavran without seeing an obvious concern for the poor, the oppressed, and the masses, which should warm the cockles of every truly liberal heart.

Trickle-Up Evangelism

I cannot explain nor even begin to understand the ways of God. Why he should send Jesus to be born in Bethlehem, the least of the towns of Judah, in a distant, poor outpost of the Roman Empire. Nor why Jesus should choose twelve such unlikely men. Nor why they, in turn, should choose to move in such unlikely circles.

Ron Sider, who has sensitized the hearts of so many in our day, said it well: "When we want to effect change, we almost always contact people with influence, prestige, and power. When God wanted to save the world, he selected slaves, prostitutes, and sundry other disadvantaged folk."[10]

More than a generation ago, Ernst Troeltsch observed, "The really creative, church-forming religious movements are the work of the lower strata.... *Need* upon the one hand and *the absence of an all-relativizing culture of reflection* on the other hand are at home only in these strata."[11]

Howard Snyder notes that historically this has been true. "Church growth has been most rapid among the poor. Sociologically speaking, the roots of Christianity have most often been among the masses."[12]

Snyder quoted Troeltsch again. "The Early Church sought and won her new adherents chiefly among the lower classes in the cities.... Members of the well-to-do, educated upper classes only began to enter the Church in the second century, and then only very gradually."[13] Tertullian could say in the second century, "The uneducated are always a majority with us." John Wesley said in 1771, "Every where we find the laboring part of mankind the readiest to receive the Gospel."[14]

In an earlier age, this was the secret of the initial wildfire success of the Anabaptists in Europe. The approach of classical Protestantism was to place emphasis on

> the strategy of converting the influential and powerful ... to introduce the new teachings from the top down. The Anabaptist approach was precisely the opposite. This was essentially a lay movement, even though most of the early [Anabaptist] leaders were trained clerics. Their method—which was not consciously adopted but represented the spontaneous urge of the newly converted to share the good news with their fellows—was spreading the word from person to person, aided by traveling missioners who spoke wherever they found hearers.[15]

Then it was the Anabaptists. *Today* it is the Pentecostals—to the amazement and dismay of many other Christians who parochially believe their own "product" is far superior.

Karl Barth reflected on what happens.

> In church history—but who really knows how it really happened and does happen?—we are given a glimpse of the power which is continually at work in new and often contradictory and interrupted but ongoing processes of growth.

Because it is *spiritual* growth, it is not a growth which we direct.

> And it will continually have ... the greatest of surprises, sometimes glad and sometimes bitter. [Our] plans and efforts will have to be *ruled by it*, not the reverse. To ... [our] own astonishment it will continually *exalt the lowly, enrich the poor, give joy to the sad and make heroes of the feeble.* The rule and efficacy of the power of this growth can never be measured, foreseen or assessed by the ordinary standards of history, even when Christians try to think of their own history in relation to that of the world.[16]

Redemption and Lift

Alongside McGavran's rich insights into "the masses and the classes," and his observation that the gospel has usually been passed from the bottom up, we must place another related concept—"redemption and lift"—a reality which may be one of the barriers to continued growth.[17]

A mission will send in teachers and doctors. Agricultural experts will teach the people to farm. The people learn about sanitation and health care. They begin to move in new circles. They cease to use the dialect and start to use a standard language. Crude and obscene talk becomes repellent to them. They do not want their children to hear it. They no longer like the old life. They are earning more and saving more. They come to have a higher standard of living. A great gulf comes to exist between those who have become Christian and their own friends.

This happens not only far away. I saw it in the aging neighborhood of my initial pastorate, First Church, in a section on the Hill overlooking Harrisburg, Pennsylvania.

A generation ago, a single woman, small and filled with enthusiasm, built a Sunday school from the children of the community. The pastor had a loud voice. People in the area said they did not need to come to church because they could hear the sermons at home with their doors and windows closed.

The music was lively with gospel choruses and songs. The dress was informal. The content earthy—very simple.

The families who came into the church began to clean themselves up. Many stopped drinking. They learned to save their money. Their children began to do better in school. They began to dream of a better future. When they graduated from high school, many went to the denominational college not far away in Elizabethtown. They came back to be teachers, doctors, nurses, and business men and women. Earning more money, they no longer wanted to live in older row houses built right on the street. They bought homes in the suburbs.

Many of their parents pooled all their resources to follow them. Many of those who grew up in the shadows of the church now wanted as much space as possible from those who had been their childhood friends.

McGavran said,

> Partly because of the experience of redemption and lift, United Methodists [or Presbyterians or Baptists or Four Square members—insert the name of your own denomination at this point] see themselves as respectable people, upper-middle-class, educated, propertied people, solid citizens.

As a result

> executives who live in comfortable homes are likely to be United Methodists. "We have others, of course, but members of our church are quite prominent in this community." The conclusion of this self-image is that, quite consciously, we add a sentence: "United Methodist church growth will naturally take place among this kind of people and should be limited to them."[18]

The irony is that the United Methodist Church began as a church of *all* people. Its roots were among the poorest of the poor. But over two or three generations, redemption and lift had done their work.

McGavran went on to say that

> these important factors affect Christians everywhere and
> while it is a positive experience (the lifting of Christians to
> higher standards of health and well-being), it contains
> some trade-offs that frustrate evangelism as usual.

The result over two or three generations is that

> redemption and lift separate Christians from their social
> roots and seal off whole denominations from the lower
> classes. When that happens, churches cease to grow.[19]

The usual phrase is "quality." So often I have heard it
stated, "We prefer quality to numbers."

Peter Wagner observed that much of our talk about
"quality" usually means "schooling." Not education, because education and wisdom may be present in those with
very little formal schooling. Often, suggested Wagner, our
talk of wanting to maintain quality is snobbishness—
holding at arm's length those who we were like but a short
time ago.[20]

We see evidence of this in the early church. Rough-and-
tumble Simon Peter, a fisherman, suddenly became worried about status. The words of John to "the angel of the
church in Laodicea" in the book of Revelation: "You say, 'I
am rich and well off; I have all I need.' But you do not know
how miserable and pitiful you are! You are poor, naked,
and blind" (Revlation 3:17, TEV).

But perhaps nowhere is it more directly stated than in
the apostle Paul's words to the knowledge-conscious
church at Corinth.

> Remember what you were ... when God called you. From
> the human point of view few of you were wise or powerful or
> of high social standing. God purposely chose what the
> world considers nonsense in order to shame the wise, and
> he chose what the world considers weak in order to shame

the powerful. He chose what the world looks down on and despises and thinks is nothing, in order to destroy what the world thinks is important. (1 Corinthians 1:28, TEV)

He reminded a group of Christians who had "become rich in things, including all speech and all knowledge" of their humble origins and urged them as he would urge us, that "whoever wants to boast must boast of what the Lord has done" (1 Corinthians 1:5, 31, TEV).

Packaging Which is Too Fancy

As a result of this lifting, said McGavran, we may develop styles which tend to hinder the entrance of other peoples.

> As generation succeeds generation, most denominations settle into cultural forms of worship usually quite appropriate to the people they have become, a dignified procedure for the worship of God. Majestic worship, quiet reverent prayer, tuneful singing, impressive organ music, and aesthetic experience characterize their worship.
>
> Since only a small part of the total community "fits" worship forms like this, mainline denominations slide into assuming that only those who like majestic worship and elevated sermons are eligible for evangelization by them.[21]

McGavran offered the questions painfully to all of us who have been "lifted" by the gospel:

> Would the Galileans have liked your liturgical life-style? Would your sermons have communicated with multitudes of the working classes in the Britain of Bunyan, or Knox, or Wesley, or Marx?
>
> To put the question in a different form, suppose you could win large numbers of the American masses to the New Life by evangelizing them in less elevated ways and engaging them in a liturgical style quite different from your present practice, ways that "fit" them culturally.
>
> Would you do it? Would you cease importing culturally

foreign music and worship into settings where these forms are not natural?

Worship must be expressed in the "heart language" of the target subculture if its members are really to see it, to appropriate it, and to be involved in it.[22]

McGavran uses an example which is a little removed from us and therefore perhaps easier to affirm.

The early Methodist Church brought blessing to millions around the world, partly because it brought people to Christ and enabled them to worship God in ways that seemed natural to them, ways that were a long step removed from the stately worship of the Anglican churches of 1750.[23]

Not Without Pain

Howard Snyder helps us realize how very difficult this may have been for the early leaders. John Wesley, though an Oxford scholar, had no patience with high-sounding phrases that failed to communicate.

Wesley never compromised his message. He never hesitated to let the gospel meet head-on the hard problems of his day. He did not reserve tough application for small groups of the converted. Among other things, "he agitated for prison, liquor and labor reform; set up loans for the poor; campaigned against the slave trade and smuggling; opened a dispensary and gave medicines to the poor; worked to solve unemployment; and personally gave away considerable sums of money to persons in need."[24]

His sermons addressed such topics as wealth, national sins, war, education, medical ethics, the Stamp Act, trade with North America, and responsibility to the king. There was no question where he stood on the major social issues of his time.

Says Snyder, "There is no combination more potent in transforming society than biblical evangelism coupled with biblical social concern—the joining of Old Testament prophet and New Testament evangelist."[25]

The question was never whether the message should be watered down. The sole question was whether it could be translated into a language and a style which the masses could understand.

I think of some of the new hymns being introduced each year. How difficult some of them are to sing! What effort they take, even for one who sang in a college choir! And I reflect on some of the criteria imposed on new music in the secular world as set forth on a KABC talk show by Toni Tenille, whose husband, Daryl, works at that for a living: It must have a singable tune which sticks in the mind. It must get to that tune very early in the score, before people turn it off in their minds.

Are we, I sometimes wonder, primarily concerned about music education? Or are we primarily concerned about eternal truths apart from which people die, *using* music as one vehicle to communicate the message? Do we therefore choose the form that communicates it best?

John Stott in two powerful pages in his *Preacher's Portrait* set forth the issue well.

J. C. Ryle, formerly bishop of Liverpool, asserted that one of the secrets of the evangelical revival in eighteenth-century England was that its leaders preached simply. "They were not ashamed to crucify their style, and to sacrifice their reputation for learning."[26]

It was Augustine who said, "A wooden key is not so beautiful as a golden one, but if it can open the door when the golden one cannot, it is far more useful."[27]

David Watson addressed the issue when he said, "Anyone can be complicated. And anyone can be trite. But to preach profound truth simply is difficult."[28]

In many and various ways God spoke of old through his prophets. But in these latter times he has spoken to us through a Son, in words so clear and simple that even a child could understand (Hebrews 1:1).

Can we who claim to be his disciples do anything less?

Toward a Theology of Wholeness

The bottom line in all of this may be that our theology has gotten off course. The real issue may well be not numbers or the homogeneous principle or fear of low quality, but that down deep we have lost sight of the wholeness the gospel intends to bring to life.

Everyone has a theology. Everyone acts out of certain basic assumptions about God and people, about the worth of a human life, about the present and the future, about hope or despair, and about morals and ethics. Every movie ever produced reflects the assumptions of those who produced it. Every book ever written, every picture ever painted—they all reveal the soul of the artist.

I had a friend who was a member in an earlier church I served. All her paintings were heavy with browns and grays. A somber note ran through all she did. Her paintings revealed much about her own mood during that period of her life.

So it is that as we labor, we act out in living terms the faith that motivates us.

If it is a selfish faith, a racist faith, or a belligerent faith, it will show through in what we preach and what we teach and in what we create around us. If it is a frantically active faith without spiritual depth, that too will be seen.

The basic questions in our look at church growth are, after all, not mechanics, but "What is our purpose?" "To what have we been called?" Not, "Are we faithful?" but, rather, "To *what* are we to be faithful?" To the Christ, to be sure, and to his dreams. And to his commands. But what does that entail? Those are the prior questions.

What kind of church did he envision? He called them "the gathered," the "called out." Called out for special tasks—his tasks.

And whose church was it to be? We talk of "my" church or "our" church. I think of a woman, one of the pillars in a church I served, who one Sunday morning asked in dismay, "Who are all these new people in *our* church?" If it is my church or your church, or even our church, it is not a church. It is simply a social club. And the world has more than enough of those already.

If it is to be *the* church, it must be Christ's church. And if it is Christ's church, then it is to be for all people. Then it carries within it a passion for those outside. Never can it be said by a member, "We are too large already." The question is not how cozy "our" fellowship is but how well we are completing the mission to which we have been called. The "movement and the magnificence" are not ours but his.

Never can we dismiss God's children with ease. We cannot shrug, "Well, Jim is a hothead anyway. Maybe the church is better off without him." Or, "The Smiths just aren't the church-going kind." Or, "With their problems, it is no wonder they aren't here."

Nor can we say, as a pastor friend who serves a large college church replied, "I think the whole concern over church growth is irrelevant. That is not my agenda."

I was recently discussing a possible vacation Bible school curriculum with Christian education personnel. The material dealt with separation from God, with such questions as fear and loneliness and God's dreams for us. One person said, "Children are not interested in questions like that. They want to talk about the things they experience in life."

I felt no particular need to defend the material. It was not produced by our denomination. But I felt I did need to respond to what had been said.

Children do experience separation because of sin. Even a young child who has stolen or lied or disobeyed feels cut off from brothers, sisters, and parents. They often turn critical and become difficult to live with when there are things within themselves which they know to be "out of joint."

Children do experience fear. The example in the material was a picture of two older boys on a school ground telling a young boy to give them money for lunch.

Growing up in industrial Lima, Ohio, during World War II, I experienced that kind of fear on the playground and in my own neighborhood many times. There was an older boy in our fourth-grade class. He had failed once or twice. He was in love with the prettiest girl in the class. She didn't notice him but she would talk to me from time to time or smile at me. If he felt she had shown too much attention to me, he would punch me in the arm. My arm was soon black and blue. I came to dread going home from school each day.

There are other fears. One young woman's parents were divorced when she was just entering high school. She finally confided to her father at age 23 that all through her early years she had one recurring nightmare. She often dreamed that she was in a large shopping center surrounded by strange people. Her mother would suddenly turn and walk away, leaving her all alone. She had evidently overheard her mother talk of leaving. And it left its mark on that young heart.

Children have more fears than they talk about.

There is loneliness in our world, a lostness with which we in our own strength are not able to cope.

A middle-aged woman who had previously lost two husbands—one through death and a second through divorce—was contemplating divorce again to escape a bad marriage. "The trouble is," she said, "I know what happens to me when I am not married. I become the kind of woman I don't want to be."

Fulton Sheen said one time, "A river must be happier than a swamp because it has banks and boundaries. A swamp is a valley of liberty that has lost its shores." Many people feel their lives are like swamps.

A mother with several small children decided she wanted to be free—to party, to be with other men, and to

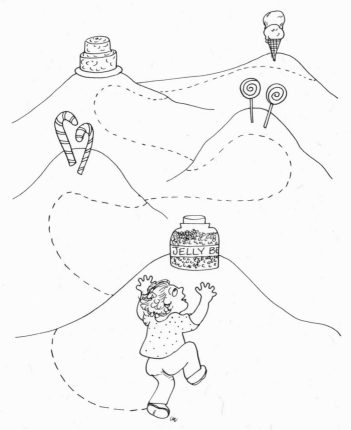

I WANT IT ! I WANT IT ! I WANT IT !

come home when she chose. She moved out of her home. It all seemed so good. But she had no employment, no means of support. Already thin, she lost considerable weight. She confided to friends that she was not able to sleep at night. She was "free" but deeply troubled and at loose ends.

A girl in her early teens in Harrisburg, Pennsylvania, was with her boyfriend and some others. It was midnight and she had promised to be home by midnight. She called her mother with her boyfriend close at hand.

"Do I need to come home now or can I stay out for a few more hours?"

The mother said, "You know how it is with us, honey. You can do whatever you want to do. You don't need to ask."

But the girl replied so that her boyfriend could hear, "That's just the trouble with you, Mom. You never let me do anything."

And turning to her boyfriend she said, "Mom says I need to come home." And she slammed down the receiver. She wanted more boundaries for her life than her mother was willing to help her have.

Separation. Lostness and loneliness. Fear. There is a looseness which leaves people—even people who have been to hell and back—feeling rootless, faithless, troubled, and not at all happy.

Meanwhile, the church, with a message of wholeness, isn't sure whether it even needs to be shared.

We mentioned earlier Peter Wagner's observation that the loss of membership in many denominations was because they had shifted their goals. "Making disciples" was no longer a priority. Other worthy social goals had taken top place. Evangelism—reaching out to lost people—has been moved to second or third place.

In a class on Church Growth, Wagner mentioned this. A leader in one of those denominations said to me at the break time, "I think he is being far too generous. My bishop would say that evangelism isn't a part of it at all. It isn't that 'making disciples' has been dropped in its priority. It doesn't even have a place."

The problem is not only with so-called "mainstream" or "liberal" churches. Those at the other end of the theological spectrum face it too.

A beautiful young woman with two small children visited our church. She sat near the back. But she was very restless, in and out several times during the service. The children seemed quiet enough. She was the one having trouble sitting still.

I visited in her apartment (sparsely furnished but neat and clean). She brought out a record with a large picture on the cover. A handsome man, he looked strong. "That's my daddy," she announced proudly, "and these are some of his sermons." She told me he was a preacher in a very conservative church. "I like his kind of preaching. I need something strong which puts it all in plain language—no mincing of words."

She talked with pride about her mother who tried to help the children do what was right and worked very hard even though they had been poor.

Then she broke into tears and said, "I guess I'm trying to be proud of my mother and feel good about her." But then she went on to say that her mother weighed more than 300 pounds, was very sloppy, and was a terrible housekeeper. She could hardly get herself around. She spent much of her time in bed or slouched in a large easy chair.

And her daddy, she went on, would preach his powerful sermons on Sunday morning and Sunday night. He could pray with deep conviction. But on Friday and Saturday nights, he headed for girlie shows. He could not leave them alone. The money they should have had for food and clothes was spent there.

She herself had led a strictly supervised life while young, traveling with her daddy and assisting in the services. But when she was old enough, she broke away. She served a hitch in the army where she fell in love with two soldiers. She went to Alaska to dance topless in a bar. She married one of the men she had met in the army, but her two children were fathered by the other man during periods when she and her husband had had fights and were separated.

Those with strong preaching, who "tell it like it is" with "no words minced," also sometimes have lost sight of the wholeness of life which is promised in Jesus Christ.

Those who have made the faith too rigid, too narrow, or too harsh, we need to remind of Jesus' statement of intention: "I have come that you might have life and have it more abundantly" (John 10:10, TEV).

For those who have let other (worthy) social goals move into the center of focus, replacing the heart of the message, we must recall Jesus' words in another context, "Seek first his kingdom and his righteousness and all these things will be yours as well" (Matthew 6:33, RSV).

Perhaps we ourselves need to come to the gospels as if for the first time. G. K. Chesterton talked of wishing he could enter his home through the second story and see it as a burglar might, as if for the first time. We need to see our faith fresh and new, to discover again its utter joy and its simple power. It may be that some of us have lived with it too long.

When we see it, then we will want to share it.

For some there are our own bad memories—as children, perhaps, or as youth. Times when the bearers of the faith unknowingly negated that faith.

A national church publication editor wrote, "Remember those revivals . . . protracted meetings they were called." In his mind flashed "staccato-paced images: . . . tightly packed country churches, hot summer evenings; funeral home fans aflutter; Bible-thumping evangelists; wasps engaged in aerial dogfights around the overhead lamps" which he says were "a welcome distraction for small children."

Without fondness he recalls "altar calls, 'invitational' hymns—mournful dirges with their last verses repeated 'just one more time' for the sake of the hesitant sinner."

What are the bad memories which linger in your mind? JWs standing like statues before the supermarket entrance with their *Watchtowers* in hand? Mormon young men in their white shirts, dark narrow ties, and dark trousers, riding on their bikes through your neighborhood confronting reluctant wives at the front door of their homes? Some radio preachers with nasal tones and simplistic messages?

A man named Jeffry Mallow, a product of the Sputnik era which produced a renewed U.S. interest in the physical sciences, now works at "science anxiety." Many in our day of scientific advance find science strange and difficult.

It may be that we need sensitive experts to work with us at "faith anxiety," with those frightened off and who need to overcome many fears and misrepresentations before they can get back to the clear, cool water, the mountain spring of renewal and refreshment.

Some poet has said,

Alas for those who never sing
But die with all their music in them.

The great Paganini presented his violin to the city of Florence on the condition *that it never be used!*

But good news is too grand to be buried.

It demands to be shared.

The Paradox of Growth

We moderns want things short and simple. In ancient times when everything had to be lettered by hand, people may have preferred long, complicated sentences. But not anymore.

It was said that President Eisenhower would never consider any problem until all the relevant information could be reduced to one typewritten sheet.

Ours is the land of the *Reader's Digest, The Living Bible* in today's most conversational English, the Whitman sampler. Keep it short. Make it simple. Move it fast.

I know a man whose job it is to shave miliseconds off half minute and minute radio and TV commercials.

Our attention span is geared to the half-hour television program. Our reading is on the sixth-grade level.

You can even check yourself out to make sure what you say reaches the masses. Use mostly one-syllable words. Keep sentences short and snappy.

And not all of this is wrong.

The apostle Paul, when he wrote his immortal letters, did not use Classical Greek. Surely if he knew the importance of what he was saying, he would have wanted it to be in the finest language available. Right? His letters were not just advice to a squabbling church at Corinth. His words were to last for centuries, to the end of time. So the form must be the finest. Right?

Wrong. Paul did not use the language of Plato and the learned. Paul wrote in Koine Greek, the language of the streets. Some of what he wrote borders on slang. His language is earthy and blunt. Some of it is so direct that at points translators have tampered with God's Holy Word to dress it up and make it more "appropriate" for reading in church. When he was raging against the Judaizers and circumcizers he said, "I hope they castrate themselves." That is hardly the kind of thing you want to blurt out over the pulpit to the average comfortable group of well-dressed worshipers after a fine rendition of Handel on a Sunday morning.

It is right that we want to present Jesus simply, in an understandable way. That part is right.

What is wrong is that in our effort, sometimes we water down his truth. We want to make him painless, to take away all the rough edges. But in so doing, we reduce the impact of what he tried to say and do.

Jesus himself went out of his way to make certain that people understood. Sometimes his problem was that they understood too well. The Scriptures tell us that "the common people heard him gladly" (Mark 12:37). They heard and they knew what he meant.

But he never softened the impact. He never diminished or minimized the message.

Nor can we.

Serve It Straight

There is a strange paradox about growth which we have touched on in this brief journey together. But we need to say it again—more directly, perhaps, in the hope that no one misunderstands.

Those churches which set out *only* to grow usually don't. Or the growth they experience is cheap and short-lived. The best, most lasting growth comes as a result of something else.

Howard Hughes had it all: wealth, fame, women—all the

finer things of life that money could buy. He was into successful businesses. He knew how to manage. Everything he touched seemed to turn to cash.

But the television story of his life seems to indicate that he was not happy. Indications are that he was obsessed with a desire for health, with a fear of germs, and with a deadly phobia that somehow the possibilities of sickness would wipe him out.

He spent his later years running from sickness, hiding from anything that might diminish or destroy him.

A segment of the whimsical television series, "Mork and Mindy," dealt with this. Mork secured a glass aquarium in which to live, safe from all the chemicals and germs which might damage health. He chose to live in virtual isolation for a short time—that is, until Mindy helped him see that in so doing he was cutting himself off.

Mork concluded, "Life is a gift. It is a sin if we return it unopened."

Health does not come by focusing on health. There are things we must do, of course. But if it becomes an obsession, health and full life elude us.

It's that way with happiness. We have long known that if you set your heart on achieving happiness and make that your supreme goal, like a butterfly, happiness will forever escape you. But go about life, and like the butterfly, it may come and land on your shoulder.

So it is with growth.

I know so many churches that have set their hearts entirely on growth. They have tried to broaden their base. They have washed from their doctrine anything that might be objectionable. They have tried to be "community churches" not offending anyone.

Do they grow? Not usually.

Why? People don't want that.

People are hungry in our turmoil-filled world for fellowship, and a faith that has direction. People want a sense of purpose, even if that purpose involves some cost.

"Nobody wants to be brave anymore," says a little sign in a printshop. "Just chief."

But we have too many chiefs. Life, vigor, and growth come as more of us are willing to be brave, to set out boldly.

Someone once said, "Love does not consist of sitting and gazing into each others' eyes, but of looking out together toward the same distant goals."

As we move into life with faith and courage, its joys will come to us.

One man who works at motivating salespeople com-

"You're not eating all your food, dear!"

mented, "Jet pilots don't use rearview mirrors."

Many churches run their business by rearview mirrors, always looking back over their shoulders, always checking to see that people are following them. They are like the leader who asked, "Where are my people headed? I must find them and get in front of them, for I am their leader."

An evangelism counselor friend in Udel, Iowa, Marilyn Koehler, comments that more athletes are challenged by Mt. Everest than by the Alleghenies. One of the secrets of Billy Graham's success is that he is forthright.

People in Jesus' day were hungry for that. They thronged to Jesus because he knew who he was, what he was about. He spoke simply, directly, and movingly, with an authority about things that mattered tremendously.

And people in *our* day are hungry for that.

A Quaker writer, Chuck Fager, recently analyzed membership statistics for the Society of Friends. He took a careful look at evangelical Friends, the branch of Quakers that has pastors, identifies itself as "evangelical," and holds worship services similar to many Protestant denominations. He discovered that they have been steadily losing members. By comparison, the unprogrammed Friends who continue the traditional silent meeting, and employ no pastors, have been gaining members.

He found this surprising, since the evangelical Friends name evangelism as a high priority while the unprogrammed Friends do not focus on evangelism. The most growth among the evangelical Friends occurred in a judicatory which spent a million dollars in the past five years on evangelistic outreach. They grew 2 percent in the year of his study. But the Baltimore district of the unprogrammed Friends had an 11 percent growth rate despite the fact that the annual budget of its intermittently active Advancement and Outreach Committee never topped $200.

One conclusion Fager drew was that the evangelical Friends, while holding some distinctive doctrines, were not sufficiently different from mainstream evangelical congregations either to attract or hold the interest of many. At least, when you join in silent worship among un-programmed Friends, you know immediately that you have hold of something different and you can decide fairly quickly whether you want to be a part.[1]

Hoge and Roozen have indicated that the churches that are growing today are not those that try to be huge mirrors of society around them. They are often those with the greatest *distance* from culture.

Many of us have it all backwards.

Many who fear growth say, "But doesn't that mean sacrificing quality? Watering down beliefs? Bringing in people who don't really understand or share our faith?"

The answer must be, "No." That is *not* what it means. That is the opposite of what solid growth demands.

One of the first times I did a study guide on Church Growth for my own denomination, I asked an artist friend to draw a cross with pieces of a puzzle putting it together. On the pieces were elements of my own denomination's heritage—things like prayer and simple living, fellowship and family life, Christian education and worship, what we call ordinances ("sacraments" to others), and a biggie for us, peace. One piece was pulled away at the base of the cross (the great commission). The challenge was that we must integrate Christ's great commission into our wonderful package of New Testament faith.

Each faith group must do that. Each denomination and congregation must become aware of what is basic, what the most important elements of the faith are as it understands its faith.

Growth comes as Lutherans are the best Lutherans they know how to be, and as Methodists or Presbyterians or UCCs are the best Methodists or Presbyterians or UCCs they know how to be.

Growth comes not as Disciples or Baptists or Mennonites dilute what they have, as they seek the lowest common denominator with the community around them.

Christ is not lifted up when that happens. God's kingdom of love and truth is not advanced in any way when bodies are simply run through a door.

We have so much to share. We do the best at sharing it when we take what for us is basic and hold to that, not minimizing in the least. Rather, we put our creative imaginations to work to say, "How with integrity can we best share the riches which have been entrusted to us? How in our lives, our buildings, our educational materials? How in our day-to-day meetings with this huge, hungry, lost humanity all around us can we make it simple enough that they will understand? Can we find some common area on which to build? some bridge from our lives to theirs? How can we make it seem winsome, warm, desirable?"

I heard D. T. Niles say one time that evangelism is one beggar telling another beggar where to find food.

That's simple enough. And that should not be offensive to anyone. We *are* beggars. Apart from our Creator, all of life begins to fall apart. We *are* able to love our brothers and sisters enough and see well enough to sense the loneliness and lostness in their lives enough . . . if we care. And if we realize that what we hold in our hands, what has been imparted to *our* lives is, in fact, bread—the one alternative to starvation and death, wholesome, life-giving, upbuilding bread.

Once we know that, we will share. And we will share with a passion what has been strangely lacking among so many fine, dedicated Christians in the decades just past.

This bread has to do with personal salvation, with lives out of touch with the one who made them. This bread has to do with family and friends—interpersonal relationships. This bread has to do with all the hard questions of our earth about which some Christians have cared so much and who, in their caring, have become diverted from other things.

John's Gospel says, "God so loved the *world.* . . ." (John

3:16) Not just the church. Not just those nice and holy. Not just the saved. But the world, the lost, the least, the ugly.

A paper entitled "Encounter" raises a most interesting and profound question: "What is the theological significance of the fact that Paul used secular terms for designating the meeting for worship and often sacrificial terms to designate the everyday life of baptized?"[2]

It suggests,

> The church fulfills its ministry only if it becomes the focus for the need of the world. All doubts, all sins, all sufferings must be remembered there.
>
> Instead of defending God against doubts and attacks, Christians are called to open their hearts and their fellowship for the agony of the world, continuously struggling in intercession followed by the question, "What shall we do?"[3]

Sometimes we forget the affirmation of Scripture, "While we were yet sinners, Christ died for us" (Romans 5:8 RSV).

George MacLeod of the Iona Community in Scotland said it so powerfully:

> "I simply argue that the cross be raised again
> At the center of the marketplace
> As well as on the steeple of the church.
> I am recovering the claim
> That Jesus was not crucified
> In a cathedral between two candles,
> But on a cross between two thieves;
> On the town garbage heap;
> At a crossroad so cosmopolitan
> That they had to write his title
> In Hebrew and in Latin and in Greek...
> At the kind of place where cynics talk smut,
> And thieves curse, and soldiers gamble.
> Because that is where he died.
> And that is what he died about.
> And that is where churchmen ought to be,
> And what churchmen should be about."[4]

The gospel dare never be reduced to a warm personal glow in the heart or right words on our lips and blindness to all the hurt and hell of a whoring world.

God in Jesus Christ has called us to far more than that.

We need them both: evangelism, *making* disciples. And a deep, mature, gutsy social dimension—*being* disciples. They both must be there in abundance, as we said at the outset, like the two reins of two horses kept in check.

Anything less is not discipleship. Anything less is not the full gospel for the full person and the whole world about which our Savior talked and lived and bled and died.

To that we are called.

Anything less is not enough.

Study Questions and Exercises

Church Growth Under Fire deals with criticisms and strengths of the Church Growth movement. But it also deals with struggles faced by every serious Christian. Therefore we have included discussion questions, Bible study suggestions, and exercises to be worked through individually or in a group.

My thanks to Marilyn Koehler, an evangelism counselor and a public school teacher in rural Iowa, who supplied many of the discussion questions.

Chapter 1

1. Write on a paper how you would feel if there were a large influx of members in your church. List your fears, hesitations, and concerns. How willing would you be to give up your job to some newcomer who might be more qualified? Would a large number coming in from other denominations threaten the climate, the witness, or the stability of your congregation?

2. Ask the pastor to share why some church leaders oppose the Church Growth movement. Discuss.

3. A Methodist minister, W. James Cowell, who heads that denomination's congregational development recently said, "The concern I have is that churches in the church growth movement have a tendency not to address tough social problems. Our commitment is not only to saving souls, but to the social dimensions of Christian life in the world" *(Los Angeles Times*, January 18,

1986, II-4). Discuss this concern. Have church growth and the upholding of a robust, faithful Christianity at times been set against each other?

4. Ask someone what these terms might mean in daily life: "realized eschatology" and "license to play heaven."

5. Look at the quote from a business textbook. Is this true of religion? If the cost of faih were minimized, do you think more people would come in?

6. Concerning Korea and elsewhere: Is it better to have large numbers of people who call themselves Christian? Even if they have a shallow faith?

7. Sometimes a person marries another thinking he or she will change the mate after marriage. Is that a sound idea? Do you know of instances where it has "worked"? Some churches feel that way about potential converts. Is that a good approach?

8. What do you feel should be the minimum requirements for church membership? Are the requirements for church membership and for being a Christian different? Should they be?

9. How has your faith grown since you became a Christian? What areas have changed? Discuss.

10. Is the change complete for you? Discuss.

11. Read Matthew 27:16-20.

12. Pray for a church faithful to Christ in his demands on our lives and faithful to his command to go, teach, win.

13. Sing "Go Forth in Faith."

GO FORTH IN FAITH

Cleda Shull Zunkel (1903 –)   George W. Warren (1828–1902)

(Repeated before stanzas 2,3,4)

1. Go forth in faith and share the gifts you hold,
2. A — wake O Church! Your he — ri — tage de — clare:
3. Go forth in joy, your wit — ness to in — crease:
4. Ac — cept your Ma — ster's pow'r and let him lead:

Go tell the Great — est Sto — ry e — ver told.
You've spe — cial — ized in ten — der lo — ving care.
When Chris — tians cease to fight, then war will cease.
The Church will grow by meet — ing hu — man need.

The whole world waits this ca — ta — clys — mic force
Sa — lute the Saints who've brought you to this place;
You have a mess — age eth — nic groups de — sire;
When mill — ions die with ach — ing heart un — fed

Which has the pow'r to change its down — ward course.
Their sound of mus — ic per — fec — ted by grace.
Their add — ed zeal can set the Church a — fire.
Go forth in faith and share the Liv — ing Bread. A — MEN.

Chapter 2

1. Someone should present an overview of the material (or several persons could each take one section). Allow time for response.

2. Consider: What does Jesus require of his church? Divide into small groups of three or four to explore each of the mandates. Assign the following Scriptures: Matt. 10:17ff.; Luke 9:1-6; Mark 16:15-16; Mark 3:14-16; 10:42-45; Luke 13:3, 5; Luke 8:9-10, 18; Luke 9:46-48. You should discover such mandates as preach, love, listen, serve, repent, be a good citizen.

3. Explore the action of Jesus in these verses. If we are to be disciples, should we also consider these actions as mandates?

Mark 1:21-22 (preach with authority)

Mark 1:35 (pray)

Luke 6:12 (pray all night)

John 12:7 (defend the oppressed or the ones who are ridiculed)

Matthew 6:5-14 (pray and forgive)

4. List four visible symbols in the sanctuary of your church. To what "eternal reality" do those symbols point? What is the church teaching by the use of these symbols? Are you pleased by the number and kind of symbols?

5. What about your faith sharing? Is there any? Do you see examples of resorting to gimmicks?

6. *Should* your church group grow? Or would it be better if yours did not grow?

7. Ask someone to take the position: "I can be as good a Christian outside the church." How do others respond to that?

8. What keeps you from faith-sharing? List some of the reasons. Discuss them.

9. Rate your church:

	Strong				Weak
Faith	5	4	3	2	1
Witness	5	4	3	2	1
Concern for evil around it	5	4	3	2	1

10. Write your vision for the church (local, denominational, and worldwide) on a sheet of paper and save it until the end of this course. You will be checking your vision following chapter 10 and have a chance to revise it if you desire. (One person could collect these and save them.)

11. Someone should read aloud Matthew 16:13-19.

12. Offer prayers for your church ... that it live up to its high calling.

Chapter 3

1. Ask someone or several to present a review of the material in chapter 3.

2. At a recent evangelism conference, Billy Graham shared with a small group in a luncheon that he used to simply proclaim Christ, seeking to lead people to "accept him." But, he confessed, "In recent years I have moved toward accepting a much more costly discipleship." List some of the things this might mean.

3. In contrast to the "Jesus Lite" gospel, examine the words of Jesus in Luke 14:25-33 and Matthew 10:32-39. Divide into two groups. Each should look at one of the above and report their reactions to the total group.

4. Examine carefully the creed, policies, and activities of your church. Place each in one of two columns according to your feelings about them at this time.

"Lite"	"Rite"

5. Reexamine the above lists. Do they reflect the biblical imperative, denominational emphasis, tradition, or culture? Or are they locally controlled and inspired? Would you feel comfortable with dropping all those which did not have a biblical imperative? Which would you retain or drop if it were left up to you?

6. Close with a prayer of thanksgiving for the leaders who have kept the church sacred and biblical in your denomination and for the disciples through the centuries who have endured hardship to remain faithful to the gospel.

Chapter 4

1. Write a corporate definition of discipleship that will apply today. What is a disciple? What do disciples do? How do they act? How can they be recognized?

2. Individually trace your journey with God from its beginning to now. List the important commitments and/or betrayals. You may want to draw it on a paper like a road with events along that road.

Do you find that discipleship requires a series of deepening commitments rather than a once-for-all experience? How can we provide simple, meaningful, yet nonthreatening experiences for renewing commitment? (E.g., through the use of foot washing, communion, and symbols such as candles, salt, and tent pegs.)

3. Have someone (or several) review the material in the chapter.

How do *you* think of Christians—as a bounded set, centered set, or fuzzy set? How can your own congregation be defined? Would a set of clear goals be a help to your witness?

4. Oliver Wendell Holmes once said, "The important thing is not so much where we stand as the direction we are going."

Write down areas "where my back is toward Christ." Some may want to share what they have written.

5. Reflecting on the story of the Green Beret, what tenets of faith do we teach our children in church and at home which are permanent conditioning? How can we "condition" for personal and corporate growth?

6. Close with the "tent peg" commitment service. It can be adapted for church worship or for outside or camp settings.

It grows out of an explanation in Mark 8:34-38 of discipleship. The phrase "take up your cross" is a translation of an idiom of the day. According to Martin E. Marty in *Death and Birth of a Parish*, the phrase was used by a Bedouin sheik when the pasture was used up in an area and he needed to move the tribe and herds to new pasture. At that point he would use the phrase which is translated "take up the cross" and the women in that tribe would go out and begin to remove the tent pegs which secured the tent. Jesus was saying, then, that to be a disciple one had to move on from the present understanding—to stretch the mind toward the mind of God, as explained in Philippians 2.

Sing of Love

From *The Brethren Songbook*, "Sing of Love," copyright 1971 by the Church of the Brethren General Board. Used with permission.

Write each person's name on a peg and (if outside) drive it into the ground lightly to be left or removed (according to the choice of each). Then form a circle around the pegs. Individually, make your own silent commitment for what you feel Christ is calling you to do in your life.

Inside a church, have pegs in a basket on an altar or table. The people may come forward and get one and return to their seats without any recognition. Put the date and a key word on the peg to remind yourself of your commitment.

Close with the song "Sing of Love."

Chapter 5

1. The work of the Holy Spirit is described in John 14, 15, and 16. Have a student come prepared to share a listing (from a reading of these chapters) of the tasks given to the Spirit.

2. The fruit of the Holy Spirit is given in Colossians 3:12-17; Ephesians 4:23—6:18; and Galatians 5:22-26. Make a tree on the chalkboard and list some fruit which is described in those passages. Divide the class into three or four groups to work at finding fruit to be placed on the tree.

3. What is your church and you trying to sell? A particular experience with Christ which duplicates what a particular group or person has previously had? Or an encounter with Jesus for individuals which will be unique and meaningful to them?

4. Two of the moods of a Church Growth person are described as pragmatism and optimism. Do you feel this is based firmly in Scripture as the mood of Christ?

Explore John 21:1-6; John 15:1-12; John 14:9-15; Matthew 7:7-11; Mark 10:29-31; and Mark 11:22-26. Give the Scriptures to six persons or divide into groups to research. Spend eight minutes on this.

5. You are a lawyer in charge of the defense of the church in Acts. Prepare an argument which will convince a worldly judge that the church is indeed equipped with power and can transmit power to others. Stage a mock court trial. Choose accusers and jurors from the group. Spend 15 or 20 minutes at this. Can you now write a defense for the power of God based on the acts of your church? Why? or why not?

6. Review the material in the chapter.

7. A minister friend commented, "In my heart, I feel that stewardship, evangelism, healing, and moral and ethical content should flower naturally from a commitment to Christ. But the truth is that we do need to work at these."

Do these areas sometimes get lost if they do not receive special emphasis? Or do you believe they follow automatically?

8. Using the drawing, talk about "Presence, Proclamation, and Persuasion" evangelism.

9. Close by recalling together some of the ways in which you make use of the research and learning available in various areas. Let students suggest how this is presently happening (in busi-

PRESENCE
EVANGELISM

PROCLAMATION
EVANGELISM

PERSUASION
EVANGELISM

ness, industry, medicine, finance, food, and entertainment). Pray that your church will be as eager to use the best that we know in our service of our God.

Chapter 6

1. Review the material in chapter 6.

Take plenty of time to discuss the points. Make sure you understand what each point means.

2. Deal with the statement that Jesus was "a Man for his Father." In what way could you validate this statement?

3. What commitment does your church ask of prospective members? to the church? to God? to themselves? Secure a copy of the vows which are repeated before the congregation. Read them to the group. Do you ask enough?

4. Do we have a fever for "trying to be all things to all people"? In what areas can we limit our vision and make it more "on target"?

5. A brilliant lawyer friend told me why he left a mainline Protestant church. He said its primary focus was on its organization. It was filled with internal politics. Its focus was on social issues without any religious undergirding.

What is your focus?

In addition to everything else, do members find answers to life's ultimate questions? What are some of life's "ultimate questions"?

6. Work alone for three minutes and write your ideas of what your church should be in five years. Then share those ideas with two others and let them share their ideas with you.

In 15 minutes agree on three important goals your church should adopt. Now take 10 minutes to list all the sets of three goals on the chalkboard. Do this without comment or discussion. Ask each one in the group to copy them to take home and reflect on this week. Return the set next week and ask each one to mark four or five goals to pass on to the church board for consideration.

7. Offer sentence prayers for the church of God in your place.

Chapter 7

1. Share any thoughts on last week's final activity. Collect the four or five goals each has indicated.

2. Divide into small groups of three people. Share the beginning of your faith pilgrimage with the other two in the group. Allow 10 minutes for this.

3. On the chalkboard or on newsprint make a listing of what motivated people to receive Christ. The list might look something like this:

> moving sermon or evangelistic meeting
> personal invitation by a pastor or friend
> church worship service
> church school
> church camp experience
> TV or radio sermon
> crisis in life (e.g., death, accident of a loved one, financial loss, illness, divorce)

What conclusions can you draw from this listing about the value of certain approaches?

4. Make a new list of motivations for people who have been members five years or less. Think about what approaches have increased the membership in your church.

What conclusions can you draw from this list? What approaches are still valid? Are some not valid because we don't use them, or because they don't work?

5. Make a personal list of groups to which you belong. Is the "homogeneous principle" one which you have used? What about your church group? Does the homogeneous principle apply here?

6. A highly educated friend said, "The reason our congregation doesn't grow is that the church is surrounded by so many Mexicans. But we are doing well. We have several attending the church and in the choir." One of the "Mexican" families in the church is really from Ecuador. The husband is a lawyer. The other "Mexicans," including the one in the choir, are from Ceylon (now Sri Lanka), the teardrop off the shore of southern India.

Discuss the drawing "People/Kingdom Blindness." Is there

PEOPLE / KINGDOM
BLINDNESS / BLINDNESS

"people blindness" in your community? in your church? Do "they all look alike"?

7. Using the drawing, discuss "Ways Cultures Relate." Discuss the melting pot theory. Which of the ways in which cultures relate does it represent?

WAYS CULTURES RELATE

GENOCIDE

DEPORTATION

APARTHEID

8. Discuss "the two blindnesses." Ask the group to suggest examples of both blindnesses in your midst and also examples of areas in which these blindnesses have been overcome.

9. Take three minutes to find three other people who like your favorite TV show. Now take three minutes to find three people who dislike food you dislike. Which is easier? To find like-

STRUCTURAL RACISM

ASSIMILATION

OPEN SOCIETY

SECESSION

nesses or differences? How does this pertain to the homogeneous principle?

10. Have someone read to the group the story of Jesus healing the blind man in Mark 8:22-25.

11. Sing a verse of the hymn "Open My Eyes That I May See."

12. Close with a prayer for sight. To see people as they are. To see God's kingdom in our very midst.

Chapter 8

1. "Church Growth means to grow up ... to grow together ... to grow out ... to grow in numbers." Has it meant that for you? Give examples.

2. Discuss the author's statement, "Sometimes there must be less before there can be more." One pastor of a rapidly growing church talks of a "false start" that often occurs.

3. Give examples of places where churches, true to the gospel, had good reason not to grow.

4. Reflect on the statement, "Yet without goals, nothing happens. Without goals we do not act. We are acted upon." How does this compare to Romans 12:2 in the Phillips translation?

5. List some ways that the church in Acts was assertive and creative, shaping the world around it. Can the church today regain its vigor? How?

6. What message did you share with someone today? How did it reflect Christ? How can you share Christ in your messages tomorrow?

7. How did the largest church in your town or area gain its membership? What program of nurture do they provide for those new members? How do they incorporate them into the life of the church? What are their plans for growth? (You might want to ask for volunteers to interview their pastor or lay leaders and report back.)

8. List the people you have invited to church this month. Underline those to whom you have shared the message of Christ in a personal way. Circle the ones to whom you have paid a personal visit. Multiply the circles by the number of people in this group. Multiply that number times the number of underlinings. (Isn't math wonderful!) Now you know how the early church grew. It multiplied. See Acts 6:7.

9. Win Arn has said that each of us knows at least 8.4 people with whom we have frequent contact and who do not know Christ or have a church home. If we invite people who accept Christ, and they invite people who accept Christ, and those people ... the church will grow. Who does the first move toward growth?

10. In closing, read John 1:35-42. Reflect on how easy and natural evangelism was in the life of Jesus and his disciples. Pray that ours may be the same.

Chapter 9

1. Explore the statement, "Evangelism is more than reciting short formulas or giving admonishing words to total strangers. Evangelism comes as one loving heart touches another—as life touches life. It involves more than words. It involves earned trust, strong ties of caring."

List the people whom you feel were instrumental in bringing you to Christ. Does the above statement seem realistic as you look at the names?

How did Jesus practice evangelism—sharing the good news that God had come to his people? Do some research on Zacchaeus (Luke 19:1-10), the woman at the well (John 4:5-30), the woman caught in adultery (John 8:1-11), the story in Luke (7:36-50).

How can we practice Jesus' style of evangelism today?

2. On Worksheet 1 identify the "communities" in your own neighborhood. Draw in the homes and label them. How might you or your church begin to reach some of these "communities"? Which is most natural for you to reach?

3. Write down the names of five close friends, relatives, or neighbors who (as far as you know) do not attend church anywhere or have never made a profession of faith. Pass the list to your left until it circulates to eight other people in your group and comes back to you. Each person seeing the list should place an "X" by the name if she or he knows that person or has some contact with them during the week. When you get the list back, note the number of X's. Do you see how networks operate now?

4. Look together at Worksheet 2. List some of the "cells" or groups that could draw others into their fellowship within the church. You will naturally think of such things as church school classes or choir. But there may be some that you do not normally think of. A group of women that get together regularly, or the youth. How could the number of cells be expanded? How could they be turned outward to draw others in?

5. How did the early church use the network approach?

6. If your church were the only church in your town or county, would your strategy be different? Some churches that started tiny grew because they acted as if there were no other group to share the good news. They took on renewed effort.

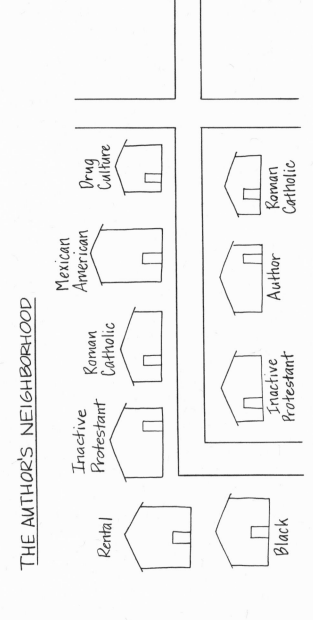

THE AUTHOR'S NEIGHBORHOOD

MY HOME AND THE "COMMUNITIES" AROUND ME

Black
Gay
Educational
Deaf
Catholic
Single
Handicapped

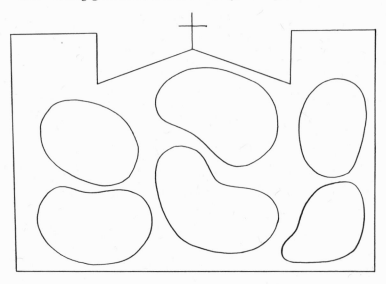

IDENTIFY THE CELLS IN YOUR CONGREGATION

7. Reflect on the networks of which you are a part. Covenant with God to find ways of "working that network" to bring people into the family of faith which you know and enjoy.

8. Sing together the song "Sing of Love" (see p. 196).

Chapter 10

1. Review chapter 10. Discuss.

2. In Matthew 9, Jesus talks of a great harvest waiting to be gathered. Note the one-to-one encounters in Matthew 8 to Matthew 12. Leaf through that section and point them out.

Even as in that time harvest was gathered slowly and painstakingly by hand, so the harvest we are to reap must be gathered through one-to-one encounters.

How does this change our method of training for evangelistic workers? Many people find crowds threatening and speeches impossible to give. But they are able to work compassionately over a cup of coffee or the backyard fence.

3. Encourage members to take time out this week to read one of the books or chapters on listening skill.

John Savage's *The Apathetic and Bored Church Member* (Pittsford, N.Y.: LEAD Consultants, Inc., 1976).

Or read material from Parent Effectiveness Training.

Or read the chapter on "Closing the Back Door" in *Growing the Small Church* by C. Wayne Zunkel (Elgin: David C. Cook, 1982).

Different ones could each report on one of the books or chapters.

4. In "My Fair Lady," Eliza Doolittle complains that she is sick of words. Could it be that the church has talked too much and related and listened too little in the past 20 years?

Or have our words been the wrong words and not the gospel?

Given your evaluation of the state of affairs, what commitment can you make at this time?

5. Is there a committee in your church presently at work which notes stress situations and alerts those involved in ministry to needs? How can the church be mobilized to serve?

6. Sing in closing, "O Master, Let Me Walk with Thee."

Chapter 11

1. Reflect on the view which places priority on winning "important people." Is such an attitude present in your church? List evidence supporting why or why not.

2. Read James 2:1-7. How does this describe the issue set forth in chapter 11?

3. Read 1 Corinthians 11:21-22, 34. Does this apply?

4. Share stories where faith came to people who were poorer and lives were lifted.

5. Do we contact people with influence when we want to effect change?

6. Does the future belong to the strong and rich? Consider Arnold Toynbee's view that history is shaped by "creative minorities." Can you think of examples?

7. Think about things in your church which may shut other, simpler people out. Could you revise or replace them without compromising what is basic?

8. Consider the poorest group in your area. If they would not feel at home in your church, could you take the initiative for beginning a church among them? Are there those among you interested in such a challenge? Do not assign it to another denomination. Are there those in your church who would like to try to "translate" the best of your denominational understanding into the "language" and forms of their life? Are there those among you who could truly love them, feel with them, and care deeply for them?

Anthropologists say that the two greatest areas of resistance in a culture are food and language. Can we enter into their life without compromising in any way the deepest of our own understanding?

9. Ask someone to read aloud "One Solitary Life" (author unknown):

He was born in an obscure village,
    the child of a peasant woman.
He worked in a carpenter shop until he was thirty.
For three years he was a wandering preacher.
    He never wrote a book.
He never held an office. He never owned a home.
    He never had a family.

He never put his foot inside a big city.
He never traveled 200 miles
   from the place where he was born.
He never did one of the things
   that usually accompany greatness.
He had no credentials but himself.
Yet we are far within the mark when we say
   that all the armies that ever marched,
   and all the navies that were ever built,
   and all the governments that ever ruled
      put together,
have not affected our life upon this earth
      as powerfully
as has that one solitary life.

10. Reflect on that life.
11. Close with prayer.

Chapter 12

1. After reviewing the material on "listening skills," talk about how you could become better listeners.

2. Spend 15 minutes right now in listing the important tenets of your faith. What teachings of your church do you feel are so important that they should not be changed? What program that you support do you feel your church should expand? If you had to pack up your faith and move it to a remote island, what do you feel would be necessary as part of the baggage?

3. In his book *Death and Birth of the Parish*, Martin E. Marty states that "while the church is historically conditioned and does not start out from scratch, many traditionally important things, if need be, could be discarded as excess baggage.... All of these could conceivably go, and the church would still be the church...."

List briefly, without discussion, those things that would need to be retained for the church to be a church in today's world. List all things suggested, even if only one member believes it important. Then have each one vote on the list by secret ballot to compile a list of the seven most important items. Indicate on the master list the votes each item received.

4. Explore this question in groups of three: How can we move toward a "theology of wholeness" by streamlining the number of commitments to program, by not spreading ourselves as thin? Does less diversity make increased intensity possible?

5. Now discuss the antithesis: How can we enlarge our witness with groups which meet the needs of all in the community?

6. Pass out the individual papers on their vision for the church written in chapter 2. Look at yours again. Are there any changes you would make? Take time for each to share her or his vision and the changes that may have resulted from this study.

7. Read Revelation 3:14-21. Paintings have shown Christ knocking at the door to the heart of a person. Note that in the Scripture, it is a church door that has shut him out.

Pray that your church will be open to Christ, to his spirit and his leading.

Chapter 13

1. Read the second chapter of Acts again. Look for results of the coming of the Holy Spirit on that group of people. What happened to them immediately and within the weeks that followed? Can you find evidence of a visible change, a message that was clear and simple, yet had great impact? Is there a sense of mission to reach people with the message? Are love and concern, praise and worship, and awareness of the power of God (Holy Spirit) expressed in everyday life? And finally, is there evidence of growth by twos, threes, families, thousands? Growth was a result of the activity of God. Call it discipleship, community, sharing the faith, or evangelism. But growth was a result. Are all of the above components evidenced in your life? the life of your congregation? the life of your denomination? Where is work needed?

2. At this point, do some verbal sharing. Begin with the phrase "Discipleship is. . . ." Complete that sentence in 30 seconds or less. Take some time to think and make notes. Let each person use the second hand on their watch. Refine your definition until you can do it in 30 seconds, and yet say something worth repeating.

3. There are three responses to the call of discipleship in John 6:66-71. Some turned away and no longer followed (indifference). Simon Peter recognized the Christ and the way of salvation. And Judas gave himself to betrayal. Challenge the group to think of attitudes which are examples of all three.

4. Test the plainness of your speech. Invite students to put the test to materials from the church and to things they themselves have written.

The Gunning-Mueller Clear Writing Institute trains persons to produce crisper writing and speech. They suggest a "Fogg index" (after a man named Fogg). You can figure your own Fogg index:

    a. Find the average number of words per sentence. (Treat clearly independent clauses as separate sentences.)

    b. Find the percentage of words having three or more syllables. (Omit plurals whose "es" makes the third syllable, as well as capitalized words and simple compound words.)

    c. Add a and b together and multiply by 0.4. The result is the number of years of schooling needed to understand you.

5. Discuss a statement by Albert Einstein: "Things must be made simple. But not too simple."

6. Fill in Worksheet 3, "Elements of My Denomination's Heritage."

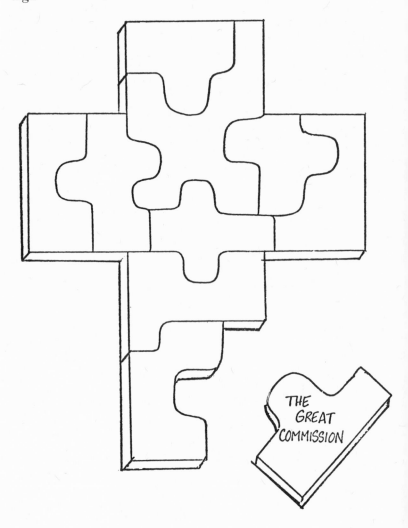

7. Discuss this statement: "Strong churches grow—churches with strong convictions, strongly held. Weak churches die. Those who try to be everything to everybody end up being very little to anybody, and nobody wants to be a part of a church like that!"

8. Let each person think quietly about Dean Kelley's question in chapter 5: "What, if anything, they are prepared to be serious about" as a church. Give opportunity for those who will, to suggest one and write it on the chalkboard or newsprint.

How many can you agree on as essential?

9. In closing, read together the words on overhead 21, "We commit ourselves anew." Sing the first verse, from memory, of "God of Grace and God of Glory."

Glossary of Frequently Used Church Growth Terms

A seminary professor once sent a manuscript to a scholarly journal. Included was McGavran's phrase "discipling and perfecting." The editor reasoned, "*Disciple* is a noun. There is no such word as *discipling*." Without consulting the professor, the word was changed and appeared in the article as *disciplining.*

A book editor wondered aloud why an author capitalized Church Growth at some points in a manuscript but not at others.

Here are a few of the terms that appear in church growth literature.

Africasia (n)—Africa, Latin America, Asia. Also *Latfricasia. Africasian* (adj.).[1]

body evangelism—an evangelism that functions out of the life of a congregation, folding newcomers back into the congregation.

church growth—all that is involved in bringing people into fellowship with Jesus Christ and into responsible membership in his church.[2]

Church Growth—". . . that science which investigates the planting, multiplication, function, and health of Christian churches as they relate specifically to the effective implementation of God's commission to 'make disciples of all nations.'" Seeks to combine biblical understanding of the way the church grows with the best insights of contemporary social and behavioral sciences. Uses as its initial frame of reference the foundational work done by Donald A. McGavran.[3] "Church Growth" is capitalized only when it refers to the Church Growth movement.

church growth eyes—according to McGavran, belong to those who see
  1. the world from God's perspective,
  2. the hand of God working in the world,
  3. the prominent dimension of human responsibility,
  4. wide differences in the outcome of Christian work,
  5. the urgent need for developing an effective strategy for church growth in every nation and among every people.[4]

church growth principle—a universal truth which, when properly applied, along with other principles, contributes to the growth of the church.

cultural assimilation factors
  A-1—slow assimilators in a culture.
  A-2—moderate assimilators.
  A-3—rapid assimilators.
  C-1—those who resist assimilation, who consciously develop a distinct way of life.
  C-2—those who are partially acculturated, who are a part of the past and the new culture.
  C-3—those who are assimilated into a new culture and experience the loss of their previous cultural identity.[5]

classes of church leadership
  class one workers—unpaid workers who concentrate their energies on tasks within the congregation.
  class two workers—unpaid workers who concentrate on reaching outside the congregation.
  class three workers—unpaid or partially paid leaders of small congregations or missions.
  class four workers—professional pastors or staff members.
  class five workers—denominational or interdenominational executives.[6]

disciple (n)—a pupil or follower, i.e., of Jesus Christ.

discipleship—a process, never complete.

discipling (v)—to disciple, to lead others to respond to the call of Christ.

discipling classifications
  D-1—"the turning of a non-Christian *society* for the first time to Christ."
  D-2—"the turning of any *individual* from nonfaith to faith in Christ."

D-3—leading an *existing Christian* into a deeper understanding of the Christian faith.[7]

discipling and perfecting—distinguishing between the task of
calling men and women to commitment to Christ (discipling) and the ongoing task of nurture (perfecting).[8]

Engle scale—an attempt to chart the phases a person may go
through from an awareness of a Supreme Being on to a decision for discipleship on through to becoming a witness
and one involved in the reproduction of disciples. Another
similar attempt at charting by Alan Tippett.[9]

Eurica (n)—Europe and North America. *Eurican* (adj.)[10]

evangelience—an approach to sharing the evangel (i.e., the
gospel, the good news) which includes research, testing, the
gathering of principles, and the application of those principles in individual and unique ways to individual and
unique settings.

evangelism—"So to present Christ Jesus in the power of the
Holy Spirit, that people shall come to put their trust in God
through Him, to accept Him as their Savior, and serve Him
as their King in the fellowship of His Church."[11]

evangelism classifications

Evangelism Zero (E_0)—evangelism directed toward
nominal church members.

Evangelism One (E_1)—evangelism directed toward one's
own culture.

Evangelism Three (E_3)—cross-cultural evangelism,
directed toward people of a very different culture.

(In some writings M-1, Mission One; M-2, Mission Two; M-3,
Mission Three.)[12]

evangelism, types of

presence (1-P)—the view of evangelism which considers
good lives and worthy example as sufficient evangelism.

proclamation (2-P)—evangelism as making the good news
known to others, whether or not conversions result.

persuasion (3-P)—evangelism as making disciples and
responsible members of Christ's church.[13] (In this view,
evangelism is tied definitionally to results.) ·

three P evangelism—a recognition that presence, proclamation, and persuasion are all essential elements of evangelism, employed in different settings or at different times.

fog—elements that prevent a church or a people from seeing and
responding to the mandate of the great commission to
"make disciples."[14]

growth, types of
> biological—children of Christians.
> transfer—members from another Christian body.
> conversion—non-Christians won.

homogeneous principle—the observation that people like to become Christians without crossing significant linguistic, ethnic, or cultural barriers.[15]

mandate, cultural—the imperative of Christian social ministries.

mandate, evangelistic—the imperative of the great commission to "make disciples of all peoples."

masses and classes—the distinction between the large numbers of common people in a culture and the leadership elite. McGavran's observation was that Christianity to be successful must grow from the bottom up, i.e., among the slaves in Egypt, the poor of Jesus' day, the common people of the Roman empire.[16]

melting pot theory—an assumption that the social ideal is to have peoples lose their cultural, linguistic, and national differences and become a new culture, usually the dominant culture.[17]

mission—God's total program for humanity.[18]

modality and sodality
> modality—a people-oriented structure, i.e., the parish, diocese, or congregation. Modalities can have "biological growth" as well as growth in other ways.
> sodality—a task-oriented structure. A group organized to do a specific task. Involves a second decision, i.e., a board, organization, or agency. Sodalities do not experience biological growth.[19]

mosaic—when applied to a community, it denotes the variety of cultural, ethnic, economic, educational, and linguistic groupings of people found therein.

pathology—identifying illnesses in the body, the church.
> terminal illnesses
>> ethnikitis—when a congregation becomes surrounded by an ethnic group or groups which it is unprepared or unable to include.
>> populus abandonmentosis (old age)—when there are no longer people from which to draw, due to declining population.
> other illnesses
>> people blindness—failure to see and respond to cultural and ethnic differences.

hypercooperativism—extreme focus of energies on inter-denominational evangelistic endeavors.

koinonitis—extreme inward focus

sociological strangulation—when church facilities are too small to permit growth.

arrested spiritual development—when a people stops growing spiritually.

Saint John's syndrome—when people, usually second-generation Christians, lose "their first love" (Revelation 2:4) and become nominal.[20]

people movements—a "multi-individual, mutually interdependent conversion," as opposed to highly individualized evangelism. Where families, groups of people, or whole villages may move together toward the Christian faith.[21]

people movements, types of

Lyddic movement—where the entire community becomes Christian.

Lystran movement—where a part become Christian, the balance hostile.

Loadicean movement—where a movement slows and stagnates.

Ephesian movement—irregular forms of the church.

web movement—extended families.[22]

pioneers and homesteaders

pioneers—longtime members of a congregation who by reason of tenure and close relationships with one another control the church. The "in" group, "old-timers," "primary group." In younger churches, the founders. Tend to be institutionally centered, survival-oriented. Tend to view the pastor as a "chaplain" only.

homesteaders—those who came later. Are not perceived by pioneers to "really belong," even when they achieve positions of official leadership. Often task- or ministry-oriented. Tend to view pastor as "leader," especially if they came in during pastor's ministry.[23]

receptivity—a point in time when people tend to be more responsive to the Christian message.

redemption and lift—the process which takes place in the lives of Christians when redemption is accompanied by better education, sanitation, health, employment, and financial situation, accompanied by separation from those who were once friends.

resistance-receptivity axis—an attempt to chart the amount of resistance or receptivity to the gospel of a given people at a given time. "Left end" peoples are those most resistant. "Right end" refers to those most receptive.[24]

search theology—committed to "seed sowing," "going every-where preaching," looking, but not committed to "finding" as an essential part of evangelism. Bumper stickers and broadcasting are, in this view, considered adequate evangelistic endeavor.[25]

sets and set structures—borrowing from mathematics the awareness that people form different kinds of categories by using different organizational principles.

> bounded sets—defined by a clear boundary. The objects are uniform in essential characteristics. Static, complete.

> centered sets—defining characteristic is not the boundary but the center. A clear boundary may exist, but there is a degree of variation. This way of understanding is more dynamic.

> fuzzy sets—one object may run into another. No clear boundary.[26]

sets and set structures as applied to Christians

> Christians as a bounded set—"Christian" is defined in terms of essential or definitive characteristics, in reference to either beliefs or a moral code. Boundary maintenance is critical. Evangelism is seen as getting people to cross the boundary between the non-Christians and the Christians.

> Christians as a centered set—"Christian" is not defined in intrinsic terms but in relational terms. The critical question is "What is the person's direction of movement in relation to the center?" A clear division exists, but it is in terms of direction and movement. Evangelism is seen in terms of people turning around, not in terms of arrival or "minimum requirements."

> Christians as a fuzzy set—"Christian" does not have clear boundaries.

spiritual gift—"a special attribute given by the Holy Spirit to every member of the body according to God's grace for use within the context of the body."[27]

theology of harvest—a theology of evangelism that assumes evangelism is not complete until the lost sheep is in the fold again, the coin is found, and the lost child is home.[28]

Notes

Chapter 1

1. Clarence Jordan, *The Cotton Patch Version of Paul's Epistles* (New York: Association Press, 1968).
2. Suggested by Dean Stendahl in a lecture at Bethany Theological Seminary, Chicago, for Second Theological Conference of the Church of the Brethren.
3. S. Charles Maurice and Charles W. Smithson, *Managerial Economics* (Homewood, Ill.: Richard D. Irwin, Inc., 1985), p. 6.
4. Karl Barth, *Church Dogmatics*, IV/2, T. & T. Clark Ltd., Edinburgh, pp. 641-676.
5. Robert K. Hudnut, *Church Growth Is Not the Point* (New York: Harper and Row, 1975), p. ix.
6. Elton Trueblood, *The Incendiary Fellowship* (New York: Harper and Row, 1967), p. 27.
7. Dietrich Bonhoeffer, *The Cost of Discipleship* (New York: The Macmillan Company, 1949), pp. 35ff.
8. Eberhard Bethge, "The Challenge of Dietrich Bonhoeffer's Life and Theology," The Chicago Theological Seminary *Register*, February 1961.
9. Albert Schweitzer, *Out of My Life and Thought* (New York: A Mentor Book, 1953, first published in 1933), pp. 48-49.
10. Dietrich Bonhoeffer, *Ethics* (New York: Macmillan Publishing Co., 1955).

Chapter 2

1. John Howard Yoder, "Church Growth Issues in Theological Perspective," from *The Challenge of Church Growth: A Symposium* (Scottdale: Herald Press, 1973), p. 31.
2. Ralph H. Elliott, "Dangers of the Church Growth Movement" *The Christian Century*, August 12-19, 1981, p. 799.
3. C. Wayne Zunkel, "Reader's Response: Countering Critics of the Church Growth Movement," *The Christian Century*, October 7, 1981, p. 997ff.

4. February 1980, pp. 27-29.
5. Lest some wonder whether he is dealing in hyperbole, William Rauscher, rector of Christ Episcopal Church in Woodbury, N.J., reports on a TV Baptist minister who plays the guitar with his toes; a Drexel Hill, Pa., United Methodist minister who dresses in a clown costume; the Arch Street Methodist Church in Philadelphia which once administered gold ashes on Ash Wednesday; San Francisco's Grace Cathedral which featured incense mingled with marijuana, acid-rock music, and recordings of wolf howls. In New York City's St. Clement's Church, barefooted worshipers were blindfolded, tossed bodily in the air, ordered to crawl on their hands and knees, and taken to a bathroom where the blindfolds were removed. There a smiling individual with toilet paper draped around his neck ceremoniously flushed away their sins. Rauscher tells of an Episcopal convention Eucharist service where the clergy consecrated bottles of Cold Duck and the congregation smoked, chatted, and joined in a snake dance while singing "Let the Sunshine In." From "Clergymen Are Turning to Gimmicks to Increase Attendance," *Los Angeles Daily News*, April 18, 1981, p. 15, section 2.
6. J. H. Oldham, *Life Is Commitment* (New York: Association Press, 1959), p. 85.
7. Karl Barth, *Church Dogmatics*, IV/3 (Edinburgh: T. & T. Clark Ltd.) p. 751ff.
8. Karl Barth, *Church Dogmatics*, IV/2, pp. 641-676.
9. Roy Larson, "Let There Be Light, Camera ..." *Los Angeles Times*, August 15, 1981, Part I-A, p. 3.
10. *Newsweek*, December 7, 1981, p. 92.
11. *Newsweek*, April 7, 1986, p. 77.
12. Michael Green, *Evangelism in the Early Church* (Grand Rapids: Eerdmans, 1970), p. 23.
13. Elton Trueblood, *The Company of the Committed* (New York: Harper and Brothers, 1961), p. 21.
14. Michael Griffiths, *God's Forgetful Pilgrims: Recalling the Church to Its Reason for Being* (Grand Rapids: Eerdmans, 1975), p. 7.
15. *Los Angeles Times*, April 13, 1981, p. 1.
16. Frank S. Mead, *Tarbell's Teacher's Guide* (Old Tappan, N.J.: Revell, 1980), p. 257.
17. Mark Fineman, "Activist Priests Openly Fight Marcos Reelection," *Los Angeles Times*, February 4, 1986, Part I, p. 14.
18. Mark Fineman, "Philippine Bishops Assail Fraud, Urge Nonviolent Protest," *Los Angeles Times*, February 15, 1986, Part 1, p. 1.
19. Albertine Loomis, "Hawaii According to Hollywood," *Youth* magazine, Volume 18, Number 6, March 12, 1967, pp. 12-15, 18-21.

Chapter 3

1. David Augsburger, "Which Call?" *Evangelism: Good News or Bad News*, from papers presented at Probe 72, an all-Mennonite Consultation on Evangelism held in Minneapolis, Minn., by Mennonite Central Committee, Akron, Pa.
2. Megan Rosenfeld, "Billy Graham's 30 years as the Evangelist's Evangelist," *The Washington Post*, January 29, 1981, p. B-1.
3. Albert Edward Bailey, *The Gospel in Hymns* (New York: Charles Scribner's Sons, 1950), pp. 123-130.

4. Donald A. McGavran, *Understanding Church Growth: Fully Revised* (Grand Rapids: Eerdmans, 1980), p. 23.
5. Elton Trueblood, *The Company of the Committed* (New York: Harper & Brothers, 1961), p. 23.
6. Karl Barth, *Church Dogmatics*, IV/3 (Edinburg: T. & T. Clark Ltd., in Ray S. Anderson, ed., *Theological Foundations for Ministry* (Grand Rapids: Eerdmans, 1979), p. 182.
7. Ed Decker and Dave Hunt, *The God Makers: A Shocking Exposé of What the Mormon Church Really Believes* (Eugene, Oregon: Harvest House Publishers, 1984), pp. 28 and 60.
8. Mike Littwin, "Black Athletes in Salt Lake City—Act of Faith," *Los Angeles Times*, December 24, 1980, Part II, p. 1.
9. Phil M. Shenk, "For the Record," *Sojourners*, March 1981, p. 9. See also John Dart, "Top Mormons Oppose MX Missile System," *Los Angeles Times*, May 6, 1981, p. 1.
10. Frank S. Mead, *Tarbell's Teacher's Guide, September 1980-August 1981* (Old Tappan, N.J.: Revell, 1980), pp. 397-398.

Chapter 4

1. Paul G. Hiebert, "Sets and Structures: A Study of Church Patterns," in *New Horizons in World Mission*, ed. David J. Hesselgrave (Grand Rapids: Baker, 1979), pp. 217-227. See also Paul G. Hiebert, "Conversion, Culture and Cognitive Categories," *Gospel in Context*, Vol. 1, No. 4 (October 1978), p. 26.
2. John Howard Yoder, "Church Growth Issues in Theological Perspective," in *The Challenge of Church Growth: A Symposium*, ed. Wilbert R. Shenk (Scottdale, PA: Herald Press, 1973), Section on "Perfecting," p. 34ff.
3. Ibid., p. 35.
4. Ibid., p. 36.
5. Ibid., p. 37.
6. Ibid., p. 39.
7. Dietrich Bonhoeffer, *The Cost of Discipleship*, translated from the German *Nachfolge* first published in 1937 (Munich: Chr. Kaiser Verlag) by R. H. Fuller, with some revision by Irmgard Booth (New York: Macmillan Company, 1949), p. 48.
8. Ibid., p. 49.
9. Ibid., p. 49.
10. Ray S. Anderson, "Living in the World," *Theological Foundations for Ministry*, Ray S. Anderson, ed. (Grand Rapids: Eerdmans, 1979), p. 589.
11. Peter Wagner, section on "The Social Challenge," class from Church Growth II, Fuller Theological Seminary.
12. *Webster's New World Dictionary of the American Language*, Second College Edition (New York: The World Publishing Company, 1970).
13. Orlando Costas, *The Church and Its Mission: A Shattering Critique from the Third World* (Wheaton: Tyndale, 1974), p. 142.
14. Donald A. McGavran, *Understanding Church Growth: Fully Revised* (Grand Rapids: Eerdmans, 1980), p. 364.

Chapter 5

1. A Lutheran appraisal of the Church Growth movement in *LCA Partners* comments that "in spite of a most welcome stress on the activity of the Spirit that appears in the literature of the Movement, recognition of the action of the Spirit in gathering the church is strangely absent." N. Amanda Grimmer, "An Appraisal: The Church Growth Movement," *LCA Partners*, August 1980, p. 11.
2. Charles Arn, Donald McGavran, Win Arn, *Growth: A New Vision for the Sunday School* (Pasadena: Church Growth Press, 1980), p. 76.
3. Donald A. McGavran and Winfield C. Arn, *Ten Steps for Church Growth* (San Francisco: Harper and Row, Publishers, 1977), pp. 1-10.
4. The basic work setting forth McGavran's understandings is Donald A. McGavran, *Understanding Church Growth*, revised (Grand Rapids: Eerdmans, 1980).
5. Karl Barth, *Evangelical Theology, Theological Foundations for Ministry*, Ray S. Anderson, ed. (Grand Rapids: Eerdmans, 1979), p. 45.
6. Ibid., p. 8.
7. Orlando E. Costas, *The Church and Its Mission: A Shattering Critique from the Third World* (Wheaton: Tyndale House Publishers, 1974), p. 134.
8. Alan R. Tippett, *Church Growth and the Word of God* (Grand Rapids: Eerdmans, 1970), p. 3.
9. Costas, *The Church* . . . p. 134.
10. Costas, *The Church* . . . p. 135.
11. See Karl Barth, *Church Dogmatics*, IV/2 (Edinburgh: T. & T. Clark Ltd.), pp. 641-676.
12. McGavran, *Understanding* . . . p. 2.
13. Howard A. Snyder, *The Community of the King* (Downers Grove: Inter-Varsity Press, 1977), p. 118.
14. J. D. Davies, "Church Growth: A Critique," *International Review of Missions* 57, no. 267 (July 1968), p. 293.
15. C. Peter Wagner, *Church Growth and the Whole Gospel* (New York: Harper & Row, 1981), p. 11.
16. C. Peter Wagner, *Your Church Can Grow* (Glendale: Regal Books, 1971), p. 12.
17. Ken Strachan developed "Evangelism in Depth." George Peters of Dallas popularized the phrase "saturation evangelism" when he was evaluating "Evangelism in Depth" and similar movements in different parts of the world.
18. For an evaluation of "Here's Life America," see Win Arn, "A Church Growth Look at Here's Life America," *The Pastor's Church Growth Handbook* (Pasadena: Church Growth Press, 1979), pp. 44ff.

Chapter 6

1. See graphs in Dean Kelley, *Why Conservative Churches Are Growing* (New York: Harper & Row, 1962), pp. 3-5, 7-8.
2. Dean R. Hoge and David A. Roozen, editors, *Understanding Church Growth and Decline: 1950-1978* (New York: The Pilgrim Press, 1979).
3. See especially Hoge and Roozen, chapter 14, pp. 315ff.

4. Colin Williams, *Where in the World?* (New York: National Council of Churches, 1963).

5. Dietrich Bonhoeffer, *Letters and Papers from Prison* (London: Fontana Books, 1953).

6. Kelley, *Why Conservative Churches* ... "Preface to the Paperback Edition," pp. viiff.

7. John Dart, "Pastors Need Humility, Schuller Advises," *Los Angeles Times,* January 18, 1986, Part II, page 5.

8. Kelley, pp. ix-xi.

9. Karl Barth, *The Word of God and the Word of Man* (New York: Harper & Row, 1956), pp. 104-135.

10. *The Best of G. A. Studdert-Kennedy* (New York: Harper & Brothers, 1924).

11. Barth, *The Word of God* ...

12. Kelley, *Why Conservative Churches* ... pp. 59ff. and 63ff.

13. Kelley, p. xii.

14. Kelley, p. 93.

15. Kelley, pp. xvii-xviii.

16. John Dart, "United Methodists Search for Ways to Reverse Erosion of Membership," *Los Angeles Times,* January 18, 1986, Part II. p. 4.

17. Alan K. Waltz, *Images of the Future* (Nashville: Abingdon, 1980).

18. Waltz, p. 26.

19. Waltz, p. 31.

20. Hoge and Roozen, *Understanding* ... p. 329.

21. Hoge and Roozen, p. 43.

22. Kelley, *Why Conservative* ... p. 343.

23. Hoge and Roozen, *Understanding* ... p. 120.

24. Robert A. Evans, "Recovering the Church's Transforming Middle: Theological Reflections on the Balance Between Faithfulness and Effectiveness"; Hoge and Roozen, *Understanding* ... pp. 311 and 308.

25. Hoge and Roozen, p. 329.

26. Juana E. Duty, "Intervention, a New First Step to Help," *Los Angeles Times,* April 16, 1981, Part V, pp. 1 and 18.

27. From a private paper prepared for the Church of the Brethren on "Declining Membership in the Church of the Brethren,"

28. Larry LaRue, "After Twelve Years, Wilkes Calls It Quits," *Long Beach Press-Telegram,* December 25, 1985, Section E, p. 1.

Chapter 7

1. Donald McGavran, *Understanding Church Growth: Fully Revised* (Grand Rapids: Eerdmans, 1980), pp. 223ff.

2. George G. Hunter III, *The Contagious Congregation* (Nashville: Abingdon, 1979), p. 121.

3. McGavran, *op. cit.,* p. 215.

4. N. Amanda Grimmer, *An Appraisal: The Church Growth Movement, LCA Partners,* August 1980, p. 11.

5. C. René Padilla, "The Unity of the Church and the Homogeneous Unit Principle," Wilbert R. Shenk (editor) *Exploring Church Growth* (Grand Rapids: Eerdmans, 1983), p. 285. (Reprinted from an article in *International Bulletin of Mission Research,* Vol. 6, No. 1, January 1982.)

6. *Ibid.,* p. 290.

7. *Ibid.,* p. 302. From John Poulton, *People Under Pressure* (London: Lutterworth Press, 1973) p. 112.

8. Winthrop S. Hudson, ed., *Nationalism and Religion in America: Concepts of American Identity and Mission* (New York: Harper & Row, Forum Books, 1970), p. 127.

9. Kevin Lahart, "Ethics '71: What Happens When the Melting Pot Fire Goes Out," *Newsday,* June 5, 1971, p. 1.

10. Russell Chandler, "Bible Translators Caught in Cross Fire of Cultural Criticisms in Third World Nations," *Los Angeles Times,* May 4, 1981, Part 1, p. 3.

11. Source: Population Reference Bureau, Interchange, September 1975.

12. Lee Lambart, "L.A. Now a Minority City, 1980 Census Data Shows," *Los Angeles Times,* April 6, 1981, pp. 1, 3.

13. Dr. Richard Landis, chairman and chief executive officer of Del Monte Corporation, to New Era Banquet, University of La Verne, March 7, 1981.

14. Sandy Banks, "Educators Face Barrier of Language," *Los Angeles Times,* January 13, 1986, Section I, p. 1.

15. Wagner, *op. cit., p.* 120.

16. Jean Strouse, "Toni Morrison's Black Magic," *Time* magazine, March 30, 1981, p. 54.

17. Ralph D. Winter, "Penetrating the New Frontiers," C. Peter Wagner and Edward R. Dayton, eds., *Unreached Peoples '79* (Elgin: David C. Cook, 1978), p. 47.

18. Based on data reported in *Churches and Church Membership in the United States: 1971,* by Douglass W. Johnson, Paul R. Picard and Bernard Quinn (Washington, D.C.: Glenmary Research Center, 1974). Available from Institute for American Church Growth, 150 South Robles, Suite 600, Pasadena, CA 91101.

19. Joel Garreau, *The Nine Nations of North America* (Boston: Houghton Mifflin Company, 1981).

20. Garreau, p. 12.

21. Garreau, p. 5.

22. Garreau, p. 5.

23. Winter, op. cit., p. 44.

24. Donald A. McGavran, *Ethnic Realities and the Church: Lessons from India* (South Pasadena: William Carey Library, 1979), p. 138.

Chapter 8

1. Peter Wagner in Leadership Forum, "Must a Healthy Church Be a Growing Church?" *Leadership Magazine* (Winter Quarter, 1981), p. 128.

2. Further revealing plates include GAMBLER, WK BLDR, TUF LFE, 7 R ENUF, SEVERED, PLN WRAP, EXQS ME, NO 1 JOCK, 4 GMA, C ME 4 ADS.

3. Robert Schuller, *Your Church Has Real Possibilities* (Glendale: Regal Books, 1974).

4. J. Robertson McQuilkin, *Measuring the Church Growth Movement* (Chicago, Moody Press, 1973), p. 30.

Chapter 9

1. James Armstrong, *From the Underside: Evangelism from a Third World Vantage Point* (Maryknoll, N.Y.: Orbis Books, 1981), pp. 50-54.
2. Malcolm Muggeridge, *Something Beautiful for God* (Fontana, 1972), p. 59.
3. From William B. Oden, *Wordeed* (Council on Ministries, Oklahoma Annual Conference United Methodist Church), p. 18.
4. *Los Angeles Times*, November 17, 1981, Part III, p. 1.
5. Boris Pasternak, *Doctor Zhivago*, translated by Max Hayward and Manya Harari. (New York: Pantheon Books Inc., 1958), p. 43. Used with permission of Pantheon Books, a division of Random House, Inc.
6. Orlando Costas, *The Church and Its Mission* (Wheaton: Tyndale, 1974), p. 138.
7. Donald McGavran, *Bridges of God* (New York: Friendship Press, 1981).
8. Donald McGavran, *Understanding Church Growth*, fully revised (Grand Rapids: Eerdmans, 1980), p. 340.
9. McGavran, op. cit., p. 337.
10. Donald A. McGavran and Winfield C. Arn, *Ten Steps for Church Growth* (San Francisco: Harper & Row, 1977), p. 24.

Chapter 10

1. "Giants Pick Up a Kicker and a Victory," *Los Angeles Times*, November 4, 1985, Part III, p. 7.
2. *World Book Dictionary L-Z* (Chicago: Thorndike Barnhart, 1979), p. 2395.
3. Martin Luther King, Jr., *Unwise and Untimely: A Letter from Eight Alabama Clergymen to Martin Luther King, Jr., and his reply* (Nyack, N.Y.: The Fellowship of Reconciliation, 1963), p. 6.
4. James Russell Lowell, "The Present Crisis," verse 5.
5. Donald McGavran, *Understanding Church Growth* (Grand Rapids: Eerdmans, 1980), p. 250.
6. T. H. Holmes and R. H. Rahe, *Journal of Psychosomatic Research* (11:213-218, 1967).
7. *The Win Arn Growth Report* Institute for American Church Growth, Pasadena, Number 10, 1986. Used by permission of the Institute for American Church Growth.
8. Published by David C. Cook, Elgin, Ill.
9. Roy E. Shearer, *Wildfire: The Growth of the Church in Korea* (Grand Rapids: Eerdmans, 1966), p. 64.
10. McGavran, op. cit., p. 251.
11. William Barclay, *The All-Sufficient Christ* (Philadelphia: Westminster Press, 1963).

Chapter 11

1. Ralph Elliott, "Dangers of the Church Growth Movement," *The Christian Century*, August 12-19, 1981, pp. 799-801.
2. Donald McGavran, *Understanding Church Growth* (Grand Rapids: Eerdmans, 1970), pp. 283-284.
3. McGavran, *Understanding* . . . p. 284.

4. Arnold Toynbee, *An Historian's Approach to Religion* (London: Oxford University, 1956), pp. 37 and 99.
5. McGavran, *Understanding* . . . p. 277.
6. Ibid., p. 279.
7. Donald A. McGavran, *Ethnic Realities and the Church: Lessons from India* (South Pasadena: William Carey Library, 1979), p. 101.
8. McGavran, *Bridges*, p. 122.
9. McGavran, *Understanding*. . . . See also "Discipling Urban Populations," pp. 314ff.
10. Ronald J. Sider, *Rich Christians in an Age of Hunger: a Biblical Study*, (Downers Grove: Inter-Varsity Press, 1977), p. 71.
11. Quoted in H. Richard Niebuhr, *The Social Sources of Denominationalism* (Cleveland World, 1957), p. 29.
12. Howard A. Snyder, *The Problem of Wine Skins: Church Structure in a Technological Age* (Downers Grove: Inter-Varsity Press, 1975), p. 44.
13. Ernst Troeltsch, *The Social Teaching of the Christian Church*, trans. Olive Wyon (London: George Allen and Unwin Ltd., 1956), I, 39.
14. John Wesley, *The Works of John Wesley* (Grand Rapids: Zondervan, n.d.), III, p. 445.
15. Donald Durnbaugh, *The Believers' Church: The History and Character of Radical Protestantism* (Scottdale, Pa.: Herald Press, 1985), pp. 74-75.
16. Karl Barth, *Church Dogmatics*, IV/2, quoted in *Theological Foundations for Ministry*, Ray S. Anderson, ed. (Grand Rapids: Eerdmans, 1979), p. 249.
17. McGavran, *Understanding* . . . pp. 295-313.
18. Donald McGavran and George G. Hunter III, *Church Growth: Strategies That Work* (Nashville: Abingdon, 1980), p. 106.
19. McGavran and Hunter, *Church Growth* . . . p. 107.
20. Peter Wagner, class notes, Church Growth II at Fuller.
21. McGavran and Hunter, p. 108.
22. McGavran and Hunter, p. 108.
23. McGavran and Hunter, p. 108.
24. Snyder, p. 172.
25. Snyder, p. 172.
26. John R. W. Stott, *The Preacher's Portrait: Some New Testament Word Studies* (Grand Rapids: Eerdmans, 1961), pp. 21-93.
27. J. C. Ryle, *The Christian Leaders of England in the 18th Century* (London: Charles S. Thynne Popular Edition, 1902), pp. 24-25.
28. David Watson, pastor of St. Michael-le-Belfrey, York, England, in the class, "Evangelism in the Local Church," at Fuller Seminary.

Chapter 13

1. From Chuck Fager's newsletter, *A Friendly Letter*, Bailey's Crossroad, Virginia. Quoted in the Church of the Brethren *Agenda*, February 1986, pastor's section. Brethren Press, Elgin, Ill.
2. From "Encounter," Vol. 25, no. 1 (Winter, 1964), Christian Theological Seminary. In *Theological Foundations for Ministry*, Ray S. Anderson, ed. (Grand Rapids: Eerdmans, 1979), p. 456.
3. "Encounter," p. 455.
4. Carl F. Burke, *God is For Real Man* (New York: Association Press, 1966) page 5.

Glossary

1. Donald A. McGavran, *Understanding Church Growth: Fully Revised* (Grand Rapids: Eerdmans, 1980), p. xv.
2. C. Peter Wagner, *Your Church Can Grow* (Glendale: Regal Books, 1976), p. 12.
3. Adapted from a definition by the Academy of American Church Growth.
4. C. Peter Wagner, *Your Church and Church Growth* (Pasadena: Fuller Evangelistic Association, 1976), p. 6.
5. Wagner, *Your Church and* . . . p. 25.
6. Wagner, *Your Church and* . . . pp. 32-33.
7. McGavran, *Understanding* . . . p. 170.
8. McGavran, *Understanding* . . . p. 172.
9. Wagner, *Your Church and* . . . handout 8.
10. McGavran, *Understanding* . . . p. xv.
11. Anglican Archbishop's Committee of Inquiry into the Evangelistic Work of the Church, 1918, in Church Growth I, a course taught by Peter Wagner at Fuller Theological Seminary, "Defining Evangelism," p. 4.
12. Wagner, *Your Church and* . . . pp. 6-7.
13. Wagner, *Your Church and* . . . p. 12.
14. McGavran, *Understanding* . . . pp. 76-92.
15. George G. Hunter III, *The Contagious Congregation* (Nashville: Abingdon, 1979), p. 121.
16. McGavran, *Understanding* . . . pp. 269-294.
17. See C. Peter Wagner, *Our Kind of People* (Atlanta: John Knox Press, 1979), pp. 45ff.
18. C. Peter Wagner in Church Growth I course at Fuller Seminary.
19. Wagner, *Your Church and* . . . p. 13.
20. Suggested by C. Peter Wagner in *Your Church Can Be Healthy* (Nashville: Abingdon, 1979).
21. McGavran, *Understanding* . . . p. 340.
22. Wagner, *Your Church and* . . . p. 35.
23. Lyle Schaller, *Hey, That's Our Church!* (Nashville: Abingdon, 1975), pp. 93-96.
24. Wagner, *Your Church and* . . . p. 29.
25. McGavran, *Understanding* . . . p. 26ff.
26. Paul G. Hiebert, "Sets and Set Structures: A Study of Church Patterns," *New Horizons in World Mission* (Grand Rapids: Baker, 1976), pp. 217-227.
27. C. Peter Wagner, *Your Spiritual Gifts* (Ventura: Regal Books, 1979), p. 49.
28. McGavran, *Understanding* . . . p. 26ff.

Bibliography

Ray S. Anderson, "Living in the World," *Theological Foundations for Ministry*, Ray S. Anderson, ed. Grand Rapids: Eerdmans, 1979.

Win Arn, "A Church Growth Look at Here's Life America," *The Pastor's Church Growth Handbook*. Pasadena: Church Growth Press, 1979.

David Augsburger, "Which Call?" *Evangelism: Good News or Bad News*, from papers presented at Probe 72, an all-Mennonite Consultation on Evangelism held in Minneapolis, Minnesota. Akron, Pa.: Mennonite Central Committee, 1972.

Albert Edward Bailey, *The Gospel in Hymns*. New York: Charles Scribner's Sons, 1950.

William Barclay, *The All-Sufficient Christ*. Philadelphia: Westminster Press, 1963.

Karl Barth, *Church Dogmatics*. Edinburgh: T. & T. Clark Ltd.

Karl Barth, *The Word of God and the Word of Man*. New York: Harper & Row, 1956.

Eberhard Bethge, "The Challenge of Dietrich Bonhoeffer's Life and Theology," The Chicago Theological Seminary *Register*, February 1961.

Dietrich Bonhoeffer, *Ethics*. New York: Macmillan Publishing Co., 1955.

Dietrich Bonhoeffer, *The Cost of Discipleship*, translated from the German *Nachfolge*, first published in 1937 by Chr. Kaiser Verlag Munchen by R. H. Fuller, with some revision by Irmgard Booth. New York: The Macmillan Company, 1949.

Dietrich Bonhoeffer, *Letters and Papers from Prison*. London: Fontana Books, 1953.

Russell Chandler, "Bible Translators Caught in Cross Fire of Cultural Criticisms in Third World Nations," *Los Angeles Times*, May 4, 1981, Part 1, p. 3.

Paul Yonggi Cho, *More than Numbers*. Waco: Word Press, 1984.

Orlando Costas, *The Church and Its Mission: A Shattering Critique from the Third World*. Wheaton: Tyndale, 1974.

J. D. Davies, "Church Growth: A Critique," *International Review of Missions* 57 no. 267. July 1968.

Donald Durnbaugh, *The Believers' Church: The History and Character of Radical Protestantism*. New York: The Macmillan Company, 1968.

Juana E. Duty, "Intervention, a New First Step to Help," *Los Angeles Times*, April 16, 1981, Part V, pp. 1 & 18.

Vernard Eller, *The Outward Bound* (Eerdmans: Grand Rapids, 1980).

Ralph Elliott, "Dangers of the Church Growth Movement," *The Christian Century*, August 12-19, 1981, pp. 799-801.

Joel Garreau, *The Nine Nations of North America*. Boston: Houghton Mifflin Company, 1981.

Eddie Gibbs, *I Believe in Church Growth*. Grand Rapids: Eerdmans, 1982.

Michael Green, *Evangelism in the Early Church*. Grand Rapids: Eerdmans, 1970.

Michael Griffiths, *God's Forgetful Pilgrims: Recalling the Church to Its Reason for Being*. Grand Rapids: Eerdmans, 1975.

N. Amanda Grimmer, *An Appraisal: The Church Growth Movement, LCA Partners*, August 1980.

Paul G. Hiebert, "Conversion, Culture and Cognitive Categories," *Gospel in Context*, Vol. 1, No. 4. October 1978.

Paul G. Hiebert, "Sets and Structures: A Study of Church Patterns," in *New Horizons in World Mission*, ed. David J. Hesselgrave. Grand Rapids: Baker, 1979, pp. 217-227.

Dean R. Hoge and David A. Roozen, editors, *Understanding Church Growth and Decline: 1950-1978*. New York: The Pilgrim Press, 1979.

T. H. Holmes and R. H. Rahe, *Journal of Psychosomatic Research* (11:213-218).

Robert K. Hudnut, *Church Growth Is Not the Point*. New York: Harper and Row, 1975.

Winthrop S. Hudson, ed., *Nationalism and Religion in America: Concepts of American Identity and Mission*. New York: Harper and Row, Forum Books, 1970.

George G. Hunter III, "HUP Clarifies Evangelism," *Global Church Growth Bulletin*, March-April 1980.

Kent R. Hunter, *Foundations for Church Growth.* New Haven, Mo.: Leader, 1983.

Douglas W. Johnson, Paul R. Picard and Bernard Quinn, *Churches and Church Membership in the United States: 1971* (Washington, D.C.: Glenmary Research Center, 1974). Available from Institute for American Church Growth, 150 South Robles, Suite 600, Pasadena, CA 91101.

Clarence Jordan, *The Cotton Patch Version of Paul's Epistles.* New York: Association Press, 1968.

Dean Kelley, *Why Conservative Churches Are Growing.* New York: Harper and Row, 1962.

Kevin Lahart, "Ethics '71: What Happens When the Melting Pot Fire Goes Out," *Newsday,* June 5, 1971, p. 1.

Lee Lambart, "L.A. Now a Minority City, 1980 Census Data Shows," *Los Angeles Times,* April 6, 1981, pp. 1, 3.

Roy Larson, "Let There Be Light, Camera . . ." *Los Angeles Times,* August 15, 1981, Part I-A, p. 3.

Mike Littwin, "Black Athletes in Salt Lake City—Act of Faith," *Los Angeles Times,* December 24, 1980, Part II, p. 1.

Donald McGavran, *Bridges of God.* New York: Friendship Press, 1981.

Donald McGavran, *Ethnic Realities and the Church: Lessons from India.* South Pasadena: William Carey Library, 1979, p. 138.

Donald McGavran and George G. Hunter III, *Church Growth: Strategies That Work.* Nashville: Abingdon, 1980, p. 106.

Donald McGavran and Winfield C. Arn, *Ten Steps for Church Growth.* San Francisco: Harper and Row, 1977, p. 24.

Donald McGavran, *Understanding Church Growth: Fully Revised.* Grand Rapids: Eerdmans, 1980.

J. Robertson McQuilkin, *Measuring the Church Growth Movement.* Chicago: Moody Press, 1973, p. 30.

J. H. Oldham, *Life Is Commitment.* New York: Association Press, 1959.

H. Richard Niebuhr, *The Social Sources of Denominationalism.* Cleveland: World, 1957.

Rene Padilla, "Evangelism and the World, *Let the Earth Hear His Voice,* J. D. Douglas, ed. Minneapolis: World Wide Publications, 1975.

Boris Pasternak, *Doctor Zhivago.* New York: Pantheon Books, Inc., 1958.

Megan Rosenfeld, "Billy Graham's 30 Years as the Evangelist's Evangelist," *The Washington Post,* January 29, 1981, p. B-1.

J. C. Ryle, *The Christian Leaders of England in the 18th Century.* London: Charles S. Thynne Popular Edition, 1902.

Lyle Schaller, *Growing Pains.* Nashville: Abingdon, 1983.

Robert Schuller, *Your Church Has Real Possibilities.* Glendale: Regal Books, 1974.

Albert Schweitzer, *Out of My Life and Thought.* New York: A Mentor Book, 1953, first published in 1933, pp. 48-49.

Wilbert R. Shenk, *The Challenge of Church Growth: A Symposium* (Scottdale: Herald Press, 1973).

Wilbert R. Shenk (editor), *Exploring Church Growth* (Grand Rapids: Eerdmans, 1983).

Ronald J. Sider, *Rich Christians in an Age of Hunger: A Biblical Study.* Downers Grove: Inter-Varsity Press, 1977.

Ebbie C. Smith, *Balanced Church Growth.* Nashville: Broadman, 1984.

Howard A. Snyder, *The Community of the King.* Downers Grove: Inter-Varsity Press, 1977.

Howard A. Snyder, *The Problem of Wine Skins: Church Structure in a Technological Age.* Downers Grove: Inter-Varsity Press, 1975.

John R. W. Stott, *The Preacher's Portrait: Some New Testament Word Studies.* Grand Rapids: Eerdmans, 1961.

Jean Strouse, "Toni Morrison's Black Magic," *Time* Magazine, March 30, 1981.

The Best of G. A. Studdert-Kennedy. New York: Harper & Brothers, 1924.

Alan R. Tippett, *Church Growth and the Word of God.* Grand Rapids: Eerdmans, 1970.

Arnold Toynbee, *An Historian's Approach to Religion.* London: Oxford University, 1956.

Ernst Troeltsch, *The Social Teaching of the Christian Church,* trans. Olive Wyon. London: George Allen and Unwin Ltd., 1956.

Elton Trueblood, *The Company of the Committed.* New York: Harper and Brothers, 1961.

Elton Trueblood, *The Incendiary Fellowship.* New York: Harper and Row, 1967.

John N. Vaughan, *The World's 20 Largest Churches.* Wheaton: Tyndale, 1984.

C. Peter Wagner, *Church Growth and the Whole Gospel.* New York: Harper and Row, 1981.

C. Peter Wagner, *Leading Your Church to Growth.* Ventura: Regal, 1984.

C. Peter Wagner, *Our Kind of People.* Atlanta: John Knox Press, 1979.

C. Peter Wagner, *Your Church Can Grow.* Glendale: Regal Books, 1971.

Alan K. Waltz, *Images of the Future.* Nashville: Abingdon, 1980.

John Wesley, *The Works of John Wesley.* Grand Rapids: Zondervan, n.d.

Colin Williams, *Where in the World?* New York: National Council of Churches, 1963.

Ralph D. Winter, "Penetrating the New Frontiers," C. Peter Wagner and Edward R. Dayton, eds., *Unreached Peoples '79* Elgin: David C. Cook, 1978.

John Howard Yoder, "Church Growth Issues in Theological Perspective," in *The Challenge of Church Growth: A Symposium,* ed. Wilbert R. Shenk. Scottdale, Pa.: Herald Press, 1973.

C. Wayne Zunkel, *Growing the Small Church.* Elgin: David C. Cook, 1982.

C. Wayne Zunkel, "Reader's Response: Countering Critics of the Church Growth Movement," *The Christian Century,* October 7, 1981, p. 997ff.

C. Wayne Zunkel, *Strategies for Growing Your Church.* Elgin: David C. Cook, 1986.

Index of Scriptures

General Index

Abortion 58
Acts 109,116,120,143,157,163,206
Africa(n) 33,46,118,134,142
African Independent Churches
   115
Afrikaner 32
Aggie 61
Aglipayan 33
Agricultural 61,166
Alabama 147
Alaska 178
Alcoholics 69,96
Alleghenies 184
Allied troops 62,64
American Church Growth (see
   Institute for . . .)
Amnesia 31
Amin, Idi 102
Amphipolis 157
Anabaptist 91,165
Anaheim 128,139
Anderson, Ray,57,66
Anglican 170
Animism 115,119
Anthropologists 50,212
Antichrist 42
Apartheid 32,36,101,102,204
Apollonia 157
Apollos 80
Aquino, Corazon 33
Argentina 110ff.
Arkansas 93
Arn, Charles 65
Arn, Win 63ff.,71ff.,151
Asian 23,33,114,118
Asia 107,142
Assimilation 102,205

Augustine 50,171
Ayatollas 160

Bakersfield, Calif. 84
Baltimore 184
Baptism 49,59,187
Baptist(s)60,84,108,110,112,
   167,185
Barth, Karl 16,26,41,66-67,
   89ff.,165
Baseball 29,71
Basketball 43,95
Batista 106
Battle of the Bulge 44
Beast, the 42
Bedouin 195
Bethel 29
Bethlehem 164
Big Mac 40
Biochemical weapons 38
Birmingham 147
Black(s) 23,36,102,108,114,
   137,139
Body evangelism 73ff.
Body language 134
Bolivia 73,79
Bonhoeffer, Dietrich 18-20,56,85
Boom, Corrie ten 5
Born again 49
Bounded sets 50ff.,195
Boxing 72
Brahman 163
British 46,169
Breadbasket 117
Brethren (see Church of the . . .)
Brooderbond 32
Brumbaugh, Wilbur 196

The Author

For thirteen years C. Wayne Zunkel served an inner-city church in Harrisburg, Pennsylvania, and for six, a 1000-member congregation adjacent to a church-related college in Elizabethtown, Pennsylvania. Since 1976, he has pastored two small congregations in the Los Angeles area. While serving them, he earned the Doctor of Ministry degree in Church Growth at Fuller Theological Seminary. The combination of Church Growth theory and hard, daily application resulted in a book, *Growing the Small Church* (David C. Cook, 1982), which has been used by congregations of many denominational backgrounds. *Strategies for Growing Your Church* (David C. Cook, 1986) applies more Church Growth principles to churches of all sizes.

During recent years, Zunkel has conducted weekend workshops in dozens of settings across the United States. In 1985 he led a weeklong seminar for Japanese pastors in Kobe, Japan, sponsored by the Japan Church Growth Institute. Before and after his Japan stay, the author spent two weeks in Korea, visiting churches, preaching, and learning.

A Church of the Brethren pastor, Zunkel has been concerned about the demands of the gospel and about the assumption by some that Church Growth means watering down the faith. This volume attempts to deal with some of the questions that arise. It is addressed to pastors and lay people who face such issues often.

Wayne Zunkel and his wife, Linda Lee (Langholf) Zunkel, are members of the Glendale and Panorama City Churches of the Brethren in the Los Angeles area. Wayne has five children.